RESIDUAL
MILLIONAIRE

Steve Fisher

PLAN A
Job/Career

PLAN B
Network
Marketing

PLAN C
Invest $
from Plan B

PLAN D
Branding,
Investing,
Giving Back

Praise for Residual Millionaire

"Powerful in hope and rich in wisdom, Residual Millionaire offers the reader proven business-building techniques from a true leader in Network Marketing. More importantly, the book provides a rare and valuable context for 'true' success, also providing the path on which all can achieve it. Steve Fisher is a courageous leader among leaders - and a dear friend!"

JAMES T. COLE
Colonel, United States Marine Corps (Ret)

"Steve has written a book that not only communicates principles for growth of a network marketing enterprise, but also connects on a level that will create a confident belief in this proven business model. Through his parable-based teaching, you will also develop a personal vision of what success looks like when pursued with integrity through persistence and a passion for helping others. This book paints a picture, if you will, of just what a life looks like described by the words, 'Well done, good and faithful servant'. Thanks, Steve!"

Kirk Newsom
Attorney, Residual Millionaire

Scripture quotations taken from the New American Standard Bible®,

Copyright © 1960, 1962, 1963, 1968, 1971, 1972, 1973,

1975, 1977, 1995 by The Lockman Foundation

Used by permission. (www.Lockman.org)

Printed in the United States of America

First Edition: October 2013

Includes bibliographical references.

ISBN 978-0-578-11827-7

Dedicated to my beautiful wife Diane.
You are the love of my life and the woman of my dreams.
Thank you for your never-ending support and love.
I love you more than anyone on this earth and consider
myself a very lucky man to get to share life with you.

In memory of my friend Byron Montgomery
A Marine, a Residual Millionaire, a True Success

CONTENT

1

FOREWORD

In today's economy, there are many people that are suffering and looking for answers to questions about career, family, success, and the meaning of life in general. Residual Millionaire provides not only a blueprint for achieving financial freedom, but also serves as a guide to help you find success in relationships, personal growth, meaning and purpose in life, and even success in eternity. In Residual Millionaire you will find simple principles and strategies that you can immediately put into action.

On a Thursday evening in 2005, I was sitting in a hotel ballroom in Houston, Texas, having been invited to hear about a "business opportunity." Not being a big fan of network marketing, I really didn't want to be there, but I had not been able to find a way to say no to the person who had invited me to the meeting because I owed him a huge favor. My wife and I had been praying for something to come along that would help us to pay for our three children's college educations, but never in my wildest dreams did I anticipate this meeting being the beginning of God's answer to our prayers!

Before the business presentation began, I met Steve Fisher for the first time and I immediately noticed that there was something different about Steve, something special. He was warm, friendly, genuine and sincere, easy to talk to, a master connector, and an all around great guy. He was one of those rare individuals who makes you feel like you have known him your entire life when you first meet him.

I soon found out that Steve Fisher was not only giving the presentation that evening, but that he was also one of the top leaders in network marketing and a man both respected and loved by many. Steve's integrity, his character, his honesty, his strong work ethic, his love for people, his humility, his selflessness, and his genuineness and sincerity embody the message of Residual Millionaire. Having experienced a level of financial success that others only dream of, Steve's message is power-packed with real-life strategies that work. Steve's team has grown to tens of thousands of associates and yet he still consistently pours his life into helping others.

As you read Residual Millionaire, you will be challenged, motivated, educated, and inspired. The book flows very smoothly and it's hard to put down! It's written conversationally and is like being personally trained by Steve Fisher. Steve's words are simple, yet his insights are truly profound. You will clearly see that the source of his strength and success is his faith in God. You will also clearly see that the two most important priorities in Steve's life are his God and his family. Steve's influence has touched literally thousands of lives for the good, and he continues to be both an outstanding leader and an inspiration to many.

God loves you and wants the very best for you. Steve's book, Residual Millionaire, is a roadmap to help you navigate your way to finding God's best for you! The map, the instructions, and the tools for success are here for you. I hope you will read the map carefully, follow the instructions, and use the tools to change your life.

I am eternally grateful for Steve Fisher. He is my mentor, my business partner, but best of all, my dear friend.

Louis Miori
Pastor - Houston, Texas

3

INTRODUCTION

Have you always wanted to have residual, passive, ongoing income, but didn't know how to get it? Do you want more out of life than just making money? Do you wonder what true success looks like and how you get there? That's what this book is about!

Residual Millionaire is not about one person. It's about thousands of people who choose a better way of creating income and a better way of living. It's about thousands of people who choose to fight for their freedom. It's about thousands of people who choose to not only find true success, but also teach and help others how to find it. It's about thousands of people who love helping people change their lives and change their financial futures. Residual Millionaire is a mindset.

I wrote this book to awaken people to the incredible lifestyle that residual income provides, to be a huge advocate for the network marketing industry, to be a how-to book for creating residual income through network marketing, to teach people how to handle the money generated, to help people believe in themselves, and most importantly to serve as a reminder of what matters most in life.

Even though I have been extremely blessed in life and in business, built a sales team of over 50,000 associates, and made millions of dollars along the way, I struggled coming to the decision to write this book and even struggled writing it! The voices in my head kept telling me things like, "You're not an author; you will not be able to write a good book, and you won't be able to keep anyone's attention." I was asking myself questions like, "What will people think? You don't have a college degree, what makes you think you can write a book?"

4

Isn't it amazing how we can talk ourselves right out of success? There are so many "voices" that speak to us, many of which are negative! Many of the voices come from within our own mind, while others come from people in our lives and media channels. It is so important that we learn to listen to the right voices, so we can live the life that we were created to live! So many people get caught in the rut of just surviving, rather than living. They live a life of mediocrity rather than making a difference. They live a life of survival rather than a life of significance. They listen to all the voices that are telling them they don't have what it takes to be successful and worse than that, they believe them!

Writing this book has been a life-changing experience for me. My hope is that reading it will be a life-changing experience for you. I want to lead you down the path to a life of freedom that will allow you to accomplish what you were put on this earth to do. I hope to guide you through the turns and detours that can make or break you. I found it hard to separate my faith from this path. I don't apologize for that. I was told that including it in this book would limit my audience and cost me money. However, writing this book was not about making money to me. I do hope that if you do not agree with my spiritual beliefs, you will still read the book and be able to pull out some nuggets that will help you on your journey to success!

I believe writing this book was something that I had to do. My goal is to inspire you to reach your full potential and teach you not only what it means to be a Residual Millionaire and a true success, but also how to get there! Turn the page and let's get started on your path to residual income, freedom, and true success. You never know where the path may lead you.

CREATED TO SUCCEED

> **True success comes from knowing your Creator and knowing that you were created to succeed.**

When we landed in Mumbai, India, it was almost midnight. As our shuttle took us to the hotel, it was so dark we could not see a thing. My dad had been a missionary to India since 1984, and I was joining him on this trip to experience what he had been doing for the last twenty years. We had five hours to sleep, and then we were heading back to the airport to fly to Amritsar, India, the city of the Golden Temple.

The next morning on our drive to the airport, as the sun was peaking over the horizon, my eyes were opened to a world I had never seen or experienced before. To put things in perspective, where I live in the Dallas/Ft. Worth area of Texas, there are approximately three million people. It is a large, thriving metropolitan area. Mumbai is much smaller geographically than the Dallas/Ft. Worth area, however, there are fifteen million people in Mumbai. Unfortunately, 68% are homeless.

As I looked at the slums of India, I was heartbroken. In some places, as far as your eye could see, there were eight-foot by ten-foot shanties that were nothing but four poles with a tarp over the top. They were connected together and under each one was a family. They had no running water and no plumbing. I had never been so heartbroken in my entire life. I couldn't even comprehend it.

The next week, when we returned to Mumbai, I met with one of the pastors that my dad had been working with for a long time. I asked him, "Why don't the people of Mumbai do something about the slums? This is your city!" He replied, "Steve, in India many believe in reincarnation. So, the people who don't live in the slums believe that the people who do were bad in their previous life, so they are getting what they deserve. Unfortunately, many of the people who live in the slums believe the same thing. They believe that if they will be good in their current life, it will be better for them in their next life." I couldn't believe it. Millions of people are stuck in a terrible situation because of a belief about themselves and about life.

This experience changed my life in several ways. First of all, it made me realize how blessed I am. Secondly, it proved to me how much our beliefs impact our reality.

When I returned to America, I realized millions of Americans live the same way. Not, necessarily, like in the slums of India, but they get stuck living lives they never intended to live because of a belief system that keeps them from success. They live in the slums of unbelief and it becomes what they consider normal.

However, in India and in America, there are those who refuse to believe the lies and choose to break free from the norms around them. They learn that they were created to succeed and that they can be, do, and have so much more.

In my more than twenty years of experience in business, I have been amazed by the number of people who are missing this most important key to success: Belief in God, belief in themselves, and the understanding that they were created to succeed. I believe it is so important, I wanted to devote this first chapter to it. I also believe it is something that ALL of us struggle with to a certain degree. We are all somewhat limited by our own minds and our beliefs about ourselves. You wouldn't believe the battle I had with myself just writing this book!

The problem that many people have today is they believe a lie. The lies can come from all around us, some intentional, others unintentional. They can come from parents, friends, teachers, coaches, bosses, religions, and, of course, our own mind. Many have been told things like, "You won't be successful, you just don't have what it takes, you are not smart enough, athletic enough or good looking enough. You are too fat or too skinny." Some have been told things like, "You are worthless, you're a loser, and you're just like your dad or just like your mom." Others have been told things like, "You will never amount to anything, you're not in touch with reality, and what makes you think you are going to be successful? People from our family aren't successful and don't make lots of money, you should just accept that."

Many are disillusioned by the voices that are constantly saying negative things about them. It's hard not to be! But it's important that you learn to listen to the right voices, voices of faith, hope, and love. It's important to surround yourself with voices that inspire you, build you up, and believe in you– Voices that cheer you on! You have to fill your mind and life with positive things and positive people.

Harvard psychologist Robert Rosenthal and Lenore Jacobson, principal of an elementary school in San Francisco, teamed up in a study that became known as the Pygmalion effect or Rosenthal effect.[1] This study revealed the phenomenon in which the greater the expectation that is placed on people, the better they perform. It was proven that the expectations and beliefs other people have about us have an impact on our success.

Students in eighteen different classrooms, from kindergarten through fifth grade, took a Harvard cognitive ability test. This test measured students' verbal and reasoning skills, both critical to learning and problem solving. Twenty percent of the students showed potential for intellectual blooming and were labeled as bloomers. This information was passed on to the teachers in each of the different classrooms.

When the students took the test again a year later, as expected, the bloomers improved more than the rest of the class. Two years later, they were still outperforming their peers. They were growing intellectually at a faster rate than the rest of the students. One would think that intelligence seemed to be the differentiator between the students' performance. However, that was not the case. The students who were labeled as bloomers had been randomly chosen by Rosenthal. The study was designed to show what happened to students when the teachers believed they had high potential. They did not score higher on the test, nor were they more intellectually gifted. Yet they became smarter than their peers. Some even had fifty percent intelligence gains in a single year.

The difference was in the teachers' beliefs about the students and how the teachers treated them. When they believed their students were bloomers, they set high expectations for their success. They talked to them differently, challenged them more and engaged in more supportive behaviors. As a result, the students' confidence levels were raised and their learning and development was enhanced.

Just as our beliefs about ourselves impact our success level, the expectations that others have of us can also greatly impact our success. It's not only important that you surround yourself with people who believe in you, but also to be the one who believes in others. Be that person who helps raise the performance of everyone around you because of your belief in and support of them.

> *"You develop millionaires the way you mine gold. You expect to move tons of dirt to find an ounce of gold, but you don't go into the mine looking for the dirt—you go in looking for the gold."[2]*
>
> *-Andrew Carnegie*

We all have strengths and we all have weaknesses. But, it's important to learn to find and highlight the strengths of those around you. The belief that you were created to succeed is not only how you change your life, but also how you change the lives of others. Believe in them, inspire them, encourage them, compliment them, and challenge them to succeed. They will rise to the level of your expectations! Your words either lead people to success or push people to failure. The great Napoleon Hill said, "Think twice before you speak, because your words and influence will plant the seed of either success or failure in the mind of another."[3]

As you mentor others by believing in them and raising their performance levels, it has a direct impact on your success. The more lives you impact, the greater your influence. The greater your influence becomes, the more lives you will impact!

> *"The greatest ability in business is to get along with others and influence their actions."[4]*
>
> *-John Hancock*

As John Maxwell says, "Leadership is influence."[5] By believing in others you build relationships, you empower leaders, you grow your network, and ultimately you change lives. It all starts with the belief that you were created to succeed and that leads to believing in others and helping them know that they too were created to succeed. Ultimately, by being focused on the success of others, this leads to a life of significance.

However, in order to lead people to success, I believe it's important to have a clear understanding of what true success is and where it comes from. True success starts with the understanding and belief that YOU were created to succeed, not only financially, but also in every other area of your life. Are you truly a success if you are successful financially but an absolute failure in every other area of your life? Hollywood would say yes, but the truth is no.

> *"I believe that being successful means having a balance of success stories across the many areas of your life. You can't truly be considered successful in your business life if your home life is in shambles."*[6]
> -Zig Ziglar

As I mentioned earlier, I don't believe I can accurately talk about money and how to be a true success without using the principles and teachings that are found in the Bible. They have stood the test of time. I will say, however, whether you believe in God and the Bible or not, you can learn from this book and the principles that I'm passing on.

I'm not an expert on the Bible, but I do know that the message of the Bible is a message of faith, hope, love, perseverance, overcoming adversity, and ultimately, success in all areas of your life. There are many promises in the Bible, but one of the greatest is if you seek God with all of your heart, soul, mind, and strength, you will find Him. What an incredible discovery it is when you find God! Once you find Him, He begins to reveal His plan for your life and challenges you to become what He created you to be. God is FOR you, not against you. Through a right relationship with Him, you become a better person, a better spouse, a better parent, a better friend, a better leader, and

12

ultimately a true success. Can you be successful in these areas without having a relationship with God? Yes. But are you truly successful? No. Success begins and ends with a right relationship with the One who created you to succeed.

The Bible says, "It is the blessing of God that makes you rich, and He adds no sorrow to it."[7] Once you know that your success originates with Him and in Him, it removes the temptation to believe that it is because of you and your greatness. In business and in life, there are not too many things that are more of a turn-off than an extremely arrogant person who talks down to everyone and spends most of their time talking about how great they are and how they are the reason for their success.

> **"It is well to remember that the entire universe, with one trifling exception, is composed of others."[8]**
>
> *John Andrew Holmes-*
> *Former U.S. Representative and Senator*

When you truly believe that you were created to succeed and that God has an extreme plan for your life that is greater than anything your human mind can comprehend, it not only gives you humble confidence, but it also creates an extreme need for and reliance upon supernatural help. It causes you to live life with a higher purpose, and enables you to make decisions that are in tune with that purpose.

We are told that when we trust in God with all of our heart, when we don't lean on our own understanding, and when we acknowledge Him in all our ways, it is then that He will make our paths straight.[9] It is a time-tested principle that leads to true success.

In today's world, success is measured by many different things. It can be measured by money, fame, houses, cars,

13

lifestyle, a college degree, titles, success in sports, power, and many other things that are irrelevant in God's eyes. That doesn't mean that any of these things are inherently bad or wrong. However, it's important to know the meaning of true success.

> God gives clear instruction for a wise man not to boast of his wisdom, a strong man not to boast of his strength, and for a rich man not to boast of his riches. He goes on to say:

"Let him who boasts boast of this, that he understands and knows Me."[10]

That, my friends, is true success, understanding and knowing your Creator. Without this, everything else is futile. God put a void in all of us that can only be filled with the knowledge and understanding of Him. Many people spend their entire lives trying to fill this void with other things, including "success." But, it's impossible. It's never enough, and this void can never be filled with anything else.

Does that mean that it's wrong to have success according to worldly terms? Is it wrong to have money, fame, nice houses, cars, lifestyle, positions, a college degree, success in sports, titles, and power? Absolutely not. As a matter of fact, as you will read in the "Money and Success" chapter, God can bless you with those things. But, apart from God, it's a winding road, possibly in a Mercedes Benz, that leads to nowhere. It will leave you feeling empty, unfulfilled, and ultimately unsuccessful.

In an interview with 60 Minutes, New England Patriot all-star quarterback, Tom Brady, was discussing the incredible success he has had in the NFL, including 3 Super Bowl rings. He had reached the pinnacle of success in life. He had a large 8-figure contract. He had a beautiful wife who was a famous model; he lived in a mansion, had all the luxury cars, and he said, "There's gotta be more than this." When he was then asked, "What's the answer," he gave a sincere, yet sad, response: "I wish I knew." It just shows that no amount of success can fill the void that can only be filled with a relationship with God, the One who created you to succeed.

I hope this book helps you become a Residual Millionaire, but more importantly, I hope it leads you to true success and if it's in a Mercedes Benz, then good for you! Let's continue down the path to find out how residual income can be a key to living a life of freedom and accomplishing your purpose.

15

Residual Millionaire
Action Steps

Do you struggle with belief in yourself? Are you allowing your beliefs about yourself or the lies of others to be a hindrance to your success?

1. Evaluate your self-talk. What are you telling yourself?

2. Write down the lies about you that others have said that you have allowed to prevent you from reaching your true potential and living your dreams. Begin to remove these lies from your thoughts and your life.

3. Write down positive affirmations and truths that you can say on a daily basis. There are many promises in the Bible and truths about you that God says. Once you believe and adopt the truths that God says about you, you stop believing or even caring about the lies of others.

4. Write down the relationships in your life that are having a negative influence on you. Begin limiting or eliminating those relationships.

5. Seek relationships that pull you up and have a positive impact on your life. Actively seek relationships with people that believe in you, inspire you, and cheer you on!

Are you actively mentoring others? (Mentoring and believing in others is a key to true success in life.)

1. Make a list of people you can mentor. Who can you have a positive impact on? How can you serve more people through mentoring?

2. Make it a point to speak into the lives of those you are mentoring on a regular basis. I suggest doing this at least weekly.

Are you seeking true success or are you chasing after things that ultimately do not matter?

1. The best way to keep yourself grounded and on the right path is to first build a personal relationship with the One who created you to succeed. Make it the top priority in your life.

2. Build accountability relationships that help keep you on the right path. Accountability partners should bring out the best in you and hold you accountable to your goals and integrity.

3. Make sure your priorities are in order.

THE RESIDUAL MILLIONAIRE MINDSET

Residual income is passive income that comes in every month whether you show up or not. It's when you no longer get paid on your personal efforts alone, but you get paid on the efforts of hundreds or even thousands of others and on the efforts of your money! It's one of the keys to financial freedom and time freedom.

My life has been changed by residual income. I, too, spent years of my life in a rut. I had a belief system that was keeping me from financial success. In today's economy, less than five percent of Americans are financially independent. Many people get to retirement age only to find out they can't retire. This book is a challenge to join the five percent and to leave the 95% percent!

Are you tired of the corporate world and the stress and time restraints that it brings? Are you tired of trading hours for dollars? Are you worried about whether you will have enough money when retirement age hits? Do you want to have multiple streams of income? Residual income is the answer to many of these questions! Residual income can create true financial freedom. My definition of financial independence is when your residual income exceeds your monthly expenses. When you have built a residual income that comes in every month whether you do anything or not, it gives you tremendous time freedom and financial freedom. I would submit to you that time is one of our most valuable commodities. I think we would all like to be Residual Millionaires.

There could be different definitions for Residual Millionaire, but here's my definition of a Residual Millionaire:

> **"A Residual Millionaire is someone who has a residual income that is equivalent to what you would be receiving on a monthly basis if you had one million dollars in the bank. At three percent interest that amount is $2,500 per month."**

In my opinion and experience, it's a lot easier to create a residual income of $2,500 per month than it is to get a million dollars in the bank!

We only live once. We all have a very short period of time on this earth. So, you have to ask yourself these questions, "What is my time worth? What was I put on this earth to accomplish? What is my purpose?" So many people live lives that they never intended to live. They live lives of mediocrity, in jobs they don't really like, working years for someone else, building someone else's dream, sometimes even with people they don't really want to work with. **There is a better way!**

Residual Millionaires are able to live life on their terms. In the morning, they have a choice to roll over or roll out. They can go on vacation any time they want and usually anywhere they want. They don't have to miss important events with their kids. They don't have to stress over finances, which, by the way, is one of the leading causes of divorce. They don't have to work with people they don't want to work with. They can choose to work hard when they want to or take it easy when they want to. They don't have to worry about being laid off. Most importantly, they own their time. They have time to make a difference and create a life of significance. What's your time worth?

Let me ask you a question: Do you want to create financial independence? Look at what one of my favorite personal development leaders of all time says:

> *"The secret to creating wealth is simple: Lower your expenses, raise your income, and invest the difference."*,
>
> *-Jim Rohn*

If you will apply this secret to your life and business, you will discover the key to financial independence and you will understand the Residual Millionaire Mindset. Focus on always keeping your expenses below your residual income and investing the difference.

There are many ways of creating residual income, such as real estate, network marketing, automated businesses, vending machines, song writing/recording, books, eBooks, investing, online marketing, and many others. Many who are building residual income today are doing so through network marketing. I focus on network marketing in this book because it has not only been life changing for me, but it's what made me a Residual Millionaire.

In many cases, those who are building network marketing businesses are doing so on a part-time basis and don't, necessarily, need the money to live on or to meet their current expenses. However, the mistake that is too often made is as they begin making money in their new network marketing business, they soon begin to wear the nicest clothes and shoes, eat at the nicest restaurants, drive the nicest cars, live in a nicer home-- You get the picture. Rather than looking at their newfound income as an investment vehicle, they simply raise their standard of living and become BROKE at a different level! I buy into the philosophy that assets are things that MAKE you money, not COST you money.

Now hear me, I'm not saying there's anything wrong with buying nicer clothes, eating at nicer restaurants, buying a nicer car, or a nicer home. As a matter of fact, as your residual income grows, you should reward yourself and your family by doing some of those things, within reason. But just be careful that you don't put yourself in a position of not being able to create financial independence.

Don't get caught in the Look Game, where you constantly have to upgrade your lifestyle to look good for everyone else. Remember, financial independence is not created by spending money, it's created by saving money and purchasing or doing things that create more residual income. It's working smarter, not harder.

The key is to not only have a Plan B, but to also have a Plan C and ultimately a Plan D.

Domenic Carlucci

Domenic

Carlucci is no stranger to having a Plan B. As a former Navy Pilot, he eventually became a Captain for American Airlines. He had been with American for 28 years when he was introduced to residual income through network marketing. He knew that the airline industry was changing quickly and his own retirement was in jeopardy. He was very interested in the idea of creating a residual income that would be a Plan B for him. Being a pilot and an Italian, Domenic did not lack confidence. However, he did not have business or network marketing experience. Domenic became a student of the business and practiced giving business presentations until he became one of the best presenters in his company.

He teamed up with his upline leaders and started sharing the opportunity. While Domenic didn't necessarily need the income, what he learned was that he loved the social aspect of the network marketing business and he loved helping other people change their lives. He took a part-time approach to his business, but was committed long-term. He knew that if he kept doing the right things over and over again, he would get the results he was looking for.

Today he is in the top leadership position in his company and is one of the top trainers. He was able to retire early from American Airlines and is a Residual Millionaire due to his network marketing business. He absolutely loves teaching others how to create a Plan B, get their businesses off the ground, and become Residual Millionaires.

> **I was surprised by how much I enjoy my network marketing business and the ability it gives me to help so many people. The residual income serves as a great Plan C to my retirement account. Above all, the personal relationships we have built have added immeasurable value to our lives.**

-Domenic Carlucci

THE RESIDUAL MILLIONAIRE PATH®

PLAN A
Job/Career

PLAN B
Network
Marketing

PLAN C
Invest $
from Plan B

PLAN D
Branding,
Investing,
Giving Back

This is the Residual Millionaire Path. Those in Plan A work for someone else and are dependent on that person or company for income. They also have very limited tax write-offs due to being W-2 Employees. Plan A can also apply to those who are self-employed. They own their own business, but they only make money in their business if they are present. It's imperative that you begin going down the Residual Millionaire Path by moving yourself into Plan B, Plan C, and Plan D. The tax write-offs alone can make a difference in your finances.

I do want to clarify that I am NOT suggesting that you quit your job or leave your Plan A. Your Plan A is part of the plan! It puts food on the table and pays your bills. One of the mistakes that people make is quitting their Plan A too soon, adding unnecessary stress and financial burdens.

Those in Plan B have started a network marketing business ALONGSIDE their Plan A. They have started the process of creating leverage. There can be a tremendous life-change at this point, an awakening to the power of creating leverage and an additional stream of residual income. As their business and residual income grows, they start to experience a whole new world of time freedom, financial freedom, and leverage. They also build relationships here that can help them in Plan B, Plan C, and Plan D.

Those in Plan C have had success and have been making money in Plan B. They are doing the wise thing by investing it, rather than spending it. They are creating more residual income and more leverage. Over time, as they follow the principles in this book, they create a synergy, relationships, and a reputation that ultimately allows them to move into Plan D and an extreme level of success, freedom and significance.

The key is to take the money that you make from your Plan B and invest it into Plan C, which can be real estate or other investments that create residual income. However, be careful in your investing. I've had some great investments that have made me significant money and added additional streams of significant residual income. But, I have also learned some hard lessons by making investments that I should not have made. As you begin to make more money, investment opportunities and people looking for investors seem to come out of the woodwork. I've learned that it's best to be cautious and have professionals handle your investments, while you do what you do best! There's an old proverb that says, "Where there is no counsel, the people fall, but in an abundance of counselors there is safety." [2]

Just imagine if your Plan B started creating $1,000 per month in passive, residual income. If you took that $1,000 per month and put it into other investments that created more residual income, after ten months, you would have over $10,000 in seed money for other investments! Plan B and Plan C begin working together to create a synergy in your finances. It's a great problem to have when your Plan B and Plan C surpass your Plan A! Plan D is simply taking yourself and your businesses to the next level by establishing yourself as an expert, capitalizing on your success even more, teaching others how to do what you've done, and giving back in a big way to create a life of significance.

There's no doubt about it, Residual Millionaires move from Plan A to Plan B, Plan C, and ultimately to Plan D. One of the keys to becoming a Residual Millionaire is understanding The Residual Millionaire Path and moving yourself through it. I want to challenge you to get the Residual Millionaire Mindset and start on your path to becoming a Residual Millionaire!

Residual Millionaire
Action Steps

Do you have residual income? Do you see the value of becoming a Residual Millionaire and helping others do the same?

1. Write down your goals for becoming a Residual Millionaire. Set a date!

2. Write down your Why. What is your purpose? What were you put on this earth to do? What is your ultimate goal?

Are you following the Jim Rohn plan for creating wealth? "Raise your income, lower your expenses, and invest the difference." Do you have the Residual Millionaire Mindset?

1. "Get SMALL!" Downsize your lifestyle in order to be able to invest and create multiple streams of residual income!

2. Instead of spending your money on unnecessary things, invest your money in other investments or businesses that create more residual income!

3. Put your plan together for moving yourself through the Residual Millionaire Path.

4. Decide the minimum amount you need to live on and the maximum amount you are willing to set aside for investments.

WHY NETWORK
MARKETING?

In today's world, working for yourself is actually the safer route, and working for a corporation has become the riskier proposition.

-Paul Zane Pilzer
World Renowned Economist, Entrepreneur
New York Times Bestselling Author of
The Next Millionaires

efore I answer the question, "Why network marketing," I think I should answer the question, "What is network marketing?" It's when a company allows you to be an independent representative (also referred to as associates or distributors) for them, build a sales team, and get paid commissions on your sales and the sales of other associates on multiple levels of your sales organization. It is synonymous with multi-level marketing and direct sales.

I believe it's also important to know that the Federal Trade Commission differentiates legitimate multi-level marketing companies from pyramid schemes. There are many legitimate network marketing companies that have been in business for long periods of time and have proven business models. Pyramid schemes, on the other hand, are illegal. In pyramid schemes, commissions are based on the number of distributors recruited, not on the items you sell. Most of the product sales are also made to these distributors, not to consumers in general. It's typically when money is exchanged and there is either no legitimate product or there is more money made for recruiting people than for selling a legitimate product.

Legitimate multi-level marketing companies have a legitimate product that is ultimately sold as a stand-alone product to the public and they don't pay associates to simply recruit other associates. Network marketing has been a viable business model for many years. Today, it is one of the fastest growing business models in the world. While many industries are struggling in this economy, the network marketing industry is seeing its highest growth levels.

Many of the most successful companies in the world have implemented network marketing into their business model. Look at these quotes from some great business leaders:

Jim Rohn
Entrepreneur, Author, Motivational Speaker

"Network Marketing is really the greatest source of grass root capitalism, because it teaches people how to take a small bit of capital, that is your time and build the American dream."

Paul Zane Pilzer
World Renowned Economist Author of The Next Millionaires

"Home-based businesses are one of the fastest-growing segments in our economy, and that trend will only continue, as the age of the corporation, which began barely a century ago, now gives way to the age of the entrepreneur."

David Bach
Author of Finish Rich

"When I read in Fortune Magazine that Warren Buffet, billionaire investor, was investing in network marketing, I decided I was missing something."

Brian Tracy
Entrepreneur, Success Expert, Author of Change Your Thinking, Change Your Life

"The future of Network Marketing is unlimited. There is no end in sight. It will continue to grow because better people are getting into it. It will be one of the respected business methods in the world."

Les Brown
Motivational Speaker

"Network marketing has produced MORE MILLIONAIRES than ANY other industry in the history of the world."

31

Patsy Glunt

In 1982, Patsy Glunt had a college degree with no immediate job offer in sight. She was introduced to a network marketing opportunity to which she quickly turned down, thinking, "Why would I ever succumb to that when I have a college degree?" However, she eventually said, "I'll try it," and here she is, 30 years later, realizing the reality of her dreams. Patsy is one of the highest paid women in network marketing and living her dream life. Today Patsy is a Residual Millionaire and has helped thousands of women change their lives through network marketing.

> *Network marketing has allowed me the freedom I would've never expected in a regular full-time job. Being a wife and mother but also having a career meant never having to sacrifice one for the other. In all phases of my life, being my own boss has allowed flexibility to wear a wide variety of hats a woman wears yet flourish in them all. I also love to watch people grow! Having a business that I can give away only enhances my experience because I can see others excel to their potential as well.*

-Patsy Glunt

While I will agree that network marketing is not for everyone. I do believe that some do not get involved because they have misconceptions and pre-conceived ideas about the industry for various reasons. I hope to address some of those in this book.

I believe network marketing is one of the best and most enjoyable ways to become a Residual Millionaire simply because of the relationships that can be built! In today's economy, it is also an incredible way to start your own business with **very little risk** or **capital outlay, low start-up costs, low overhead**, and, in most cases, **no employees, no inventory**, and **no rent!** The leverage that can be created by building a successful network marketing business is amazing.

THE POWER OF LEVERAGE

So many people spend their entire lives trading time for money, what's called linear income, hours for dollars. Many spend their lives working for someone else and, therefore, don't own their time. I think if most people understood the power of The Residual Millionaire Path and creating residual income through leverage, they would be much more inclined to do what they have to do to get it.

Stefan Rodriguez

Stefan
Rodriguez was simply not interested in doing anything else. He had good reason, or so he thought. Stefan had been approached with network marketing opportunities three different times, gaining little to no interest from him. He was already working a full-time career as an assistant manager at Walmart and had kept a part-time job to help make ends meet. "I didn't have the time or money to start a network marketing business," Stefan says, "Then I realized that was the very reason I needed to." Following that epiphany, Stefan took a closer look. He was attracted by the opportunity to create residual income and believed he could easily make an extra $500 per month. Indeed he did, and much more! He jumped in headfirst and added yet another thing on his already full plate of family and two separate jobs. Six months after starting his part-time network marketing business, Stefan was able to surpass his Walmart salary that he had worked more than nine years to achieve. Two years later, and at the young age of twenty-eight years old, Stefan replaced his income from both of his jobs and fired his bosses! Stefan is now a Residual Millionaire and full-time in network marketing.

Before building a network marketing business, he didn't own a home, his credit cards were maxed out, and he had several car notes he was paying on. Since then, he purchased his first home, has several new paid for cars and has enjoyed many incredible vacations with his family and friends that he didn't have the time or money to take before. Now Stefan's passion is helping others experience the same life-changing, residual lifestyle that he has.

> *I meet many who live as I once did. They work constantly and never find time to enjoy life. I emphasize the simplicity of network marketing so they know it's possible for common people to achieve success. But I also particularly stress that the reasons they give for not making a change and building a network marketing business are the very reasons they need to do so. Whether part-time or spare-time, one just needs to get started. Breaking out of the trading-hours-for-dollars cycle will create a comfortable and exciting lifestyle for your family and for generations to come.*

-Stefan Rodriguez

With this simple illustration, you can begin to understand what happens as you build a successful network marketing team. I tell new associates they should get their top three to five prospects in front of the information within the first 24-48 hours. Create urgency! Urgency is critical to success. Procrastination is the enemy of success!

By sponsoring three to five associates immediately, you not only get your business off to a great start, but you start the process of creating leverage. You are no longer the only one adding customers to your business. By helping your three to five associates get their three to five associates immediately, this quickly gives you nine to twenty-five people on your team who are also gathering customers, sponsoring associates, and adding hours to your business.

Think about this... If you are the only one working your business and you are working three to five hours per week, then you only have three to five hours per week being worked in your business. However, if you have twenty-five people on your team working three to five hours per week, then you have 75-125 hours per week being worked in your business. Just imagine if those twenty-five each sponsor three associates, that's seventy-five people working three to five hours per week in your business. That means you would have 225-375 hours per week being worked in your business.

Let's take it one step further... Let's say those seventy-five each sponsor three. That would be two hundred and twenty-five people working three to five hours per week in your business. That means you would have 675-1,125 hours per week being worked in your business! It would be impossible for you to put that many hours into your business by yourself. You have created leverage and started a process of duplication that, if followed and taught properly, will lead to total financial freedom and time freedom.

Are you beginning to understand the importance and the power of creating leverage through network marketing? You can see how powerful it is with these small numbers. Just imagine how powerful this becomes when you have thousands of people on your team. That is some serious leverage! In my opinion, it's crazy not to be building leverage through network marketing!

> *"The first six months others thought I was crazy. The second six months I thought I was crazy. Now I think everyone who doesn't do this is crazy!"*
>
> *-Jay Veal*
> *Entrepreneur*
> *Author of The Little Book of Network Marketing*
> *and 91 Days To Greatness*

The Rewards of Network Marketing

The personal development that can also be gained through network marketing, in my opinion, is second to none and incomparable to any other business or job. You will certainly get your "PhD in People." **The relationships and time freedom that can be created are priceless.** I have to pinch myself everyday. I just can't believe the life I get to live because of the success of our network marketing business and the residual income we have created. Residual income is worth the fight! As my friend, Jerry Scribner, says, "Residual income ROCKS!"

Odds are that you are not going to become a Residual Millionaire by having an employee mindset. It is critical that you understand how to begin creating leverage. Network marketing allows you to multiply your efforts, your relationships, your time, and your income. It can be an incredible vehicle to create the lifestyle that you want.

37

Ryan Morris

Ryan
Morris learned at a young age the rewards of building a network marketing business. After graduating from the University of Texas, he was hired with a local bank in Austin, TX. Ryan met every goal the bank set for him for three years and in those three years only received a three percent raise. He was highly frustrated with this and was beginning to see that he was on the wrong path. His mom, Martha Troy, who, by the way, is also a Residual Millionaire, was very used to residual income from real estate. She had many rental properties and was also creating residual income through network marketing. She introduced Ryan to residual income through network marketing when he was twenty-five years old. It would ultimately be a business that would set him free financially.

However, it would not be easy. Being young brings its own obstacles to a network marketing business. Ryan did not have instant success and experienced many frustrations. He had a very hard time getting his new business off the ground. However, he kept plugging into the corporate events and trainings. He sought out advice and leadership from top money earners. He became a student of network marketing and even got a personal coach. He was determined to build a successful business, to be one of the top income earners in his company, and live the life of his dreams. Being young and single also has advantages. Ryan was able to devote a lot of time and effort to the success of his business. He built a great team of young guns that has literally exploded Ryan's organization to over six thousand associates. Today, Ryan is one of the top income-earners in his company, has a six-figure income, and is a Residual Millionaire. He loves not having to report to a boss and meet monthly quotas. But even more than that, he loves that he is able to give himself raises and be in control of his own destiny!

> *Residual Income gives us choices in life. Because of my network marketing business, I have had the freedom to earn significant passive residual income, travel the world, and not be tied down to a job!*

-Ryan Morris

While the rewards of building a successful network marketing business can be extraordinary. The fact is it's just like any other business. Building a successful network marketing business takes time, commitment, grit, work, a fight, passion, belief, and a strong desire to succeed.

I have found there are some great companies that have proven track records, credibility, integrity, an incredible support system in place, and lucrative compensation plans that have been proven over a long period of time. I suggest you choose a company that has all of that in place. I also suggest you choose a company that has a product that makes sense for you and many others, is habitually purchased, and is RECESSION-PROOF!

You should also choose a sponsor who will be committed to YOUR success, committed long-term, and not someone who jumps from opportunity to opportunity or tries to do several network marketing businesses at once. Would you want your doctor to also be your banker and your real estate agent? I don't think so. Be wise in who you hitch your wagon to, both in the company and in your sponsor. Remember, this is a business decision and should be made accordingly.

While network marketing is a business that can ultimately give you your time back, you are going to have to give it some time before you get yours back! Anytime someone talks about quick, easy riches, I get a red flag. Typically, it takes a tremendous amount of effort and time to build a successful network marketing business that will pay you significant residual income for a long period of time. However, once you have built it, there is nothing like it. In my opinion, it can be the most rewarding business on the planet, not only from a financial perspective, but also from a relationship and time freedom perspective. It's one thing to have money, it's another to own your time, have lots of friends, and have money!

Donny

Anderson

Donny Anderson knows the value of owning his time. As a Vice President with a major international corporation, he was traveling all over North and South America. He began to have severe stomach problems that were determined to be from stress. He and his wife, Susan, decided it was time for him to leave the corporate rat race. Susan had always been in education as a teacher and Donny's background was business and marketing. They found a supplemental education franchise that matched both their strengths. Even though they were great businesses, Donny and Susan had almost $2,000,000 invested in their three franchises. They also had a huge monthly overhead of $75,000. They were making good money with their franchises when they were introduced to residual income through network marketing. It made sense to them and they were attracted to the residual income side of the business. They got started immediately by building a team of great leaders.

They soon fell in love with their network marketing business and sold their franchises one year later, once again removing a level of stress from their lives. They loved that they had no huge capital outlay, no large overhead expenses, no inventory, and no employees! Donny had built up a significant sphere of influence over the years and was able to capitalize on that with his network marketing business. He began showing his fellow entrepreneurs how they could build a network that would create leverage and ultimately create passive, residual income. Today Donny and Susan are Residual Millionaires and love helping others see the value of residual income through network marketing.

> *Because of our network marketing business, we live stress-free lives and have the financial freedom and the time freedom to enjoy our retirement years and our grandchildren. It is better than a pension plan that may not be there or worrying about what the stock market is going to do! Our residual income and the relationships that we have created have allowed us to have a retirement we once only dreamed of.*

-Donny Anderson

The opportunity to help people change their lives and their financial future can be overwhelmingly rewarding. **Be sure you look at the big picture of network marketing.** Understand that it can be a vehicle that will create more investment income for you, which will ultimately help you create financial independence. Be careful who you listen to and be sure you judge the network marketing industry with valid information and experience. There are not too many things in life more rewarding than playing a part in changing someone's life and there are not too many businesses that can give you that opportunity, like network marketing can.

Residual Millionaire
Action Steps

Are you taking advantage of the tremendous leverage that can be created through network marketing? Why not get this stream of income coming into your bank account in a big way and use it to create other streams of income?

1. Find a product that you can be passionate about, is recession-proof, and makes sense to many.

2. Do your research and find a legitimate company that has a proven track record, leadership you can believe in, and a system that enables you to succeed.

3. Find a sponsor that will be an asset to you and committed to your success.

4. Be committed to building your network marketing business over time, even if it's part-time.

5. Find others who want to change their lives with residual income, introduce them to your company, and focus on their success. Build a championship team!

AN "AMERICAN" STORY

If this doesn't have to work for you like it had to work for me... PRETEND!

I have been extremely blessed through network marketing, not only financially, but in many other ways as well. I have also learned a lot along the way. However, sometimes people view leaders like myself in the wrong light because they don't understand what we've been through to get to where we are. They don't understand that we go through the same challenges that everyone else does. I hope this story will help you and give you the confidence to push through to success in your business.

So that you can better understand where I'm coming from, I want to share my background with you. I grew up in Florida, the son of a Baptist pastor. My dad was a "stud" football player at Baylor University in 1956-57 when they won the Sugar Bowl by beating the University of Tennessee. (Sorry Cousins, I had to put that in here!)

Dad was always an incredible athlete. He came from a broken home and grew up without a dad, but he had influences in his life that led him not only to success in sports, but also to a very deep relationship with God. He has always been a great dad to me and I have always been thankful that I grew up in a

44

Christian home where my parents believed in me, respected me, disciplined me, and guided me through life from a Christian perspective. They encouraged me to be the best that I could be and they always encouraged me in anything that I pursued, anything that was worth pursuing that is. Most importantly, they instilled values in me that have carried me through life and allowed me to have success at home with my family and in business.

My parents raised me to love people. There were very few Sundays that went by that we didn't have different families to our home for Sunday lunch. My mom is a great Southern cook and it is always a special event to sit at her table. This love of people played a huge role in my business success. They raised me to respect people and to remember where and from whom my success comes.

Even though I grew up in a great home, things haven't always been perfect for me. I didn't go to college, but instead jumped right into the work force. I started out as a baggage-handler at American Airlines when I was 19 years old.

My wife, Diane, and I were married at a very young age and had our first child, Lauren, when I was twenty-two and Diane was twenty-one. I worked extremely hard in the Texas heat and cold to provide for my young family. I didn't make much money back then and I often look back and wonder how we even survived!

I worked my way up with American by becoming a crew chief on the ramp and then crossed union lines and went into management as a customer service manager. Have you ever tried to cross union lines and manage the union that you used to be a part of? It's not for the weak at heart!

It was then that I gained a lot of experience in all of the different areas of American Airlines. When 9/11/01 happened, I was a manager over the ticket counter at Dallas/Ft. Worth Airport... A day I will never forget.

Ultimately a job became available at the American Airlines Corporate Headquarters that caught my attention. I put in my application and was able to beat out many who had college degrees and even MBA's. I was hired as an analyst of airport operations for American. For a while, I really enjoyed my new position and career. I had never experienced corporate America at that level before and it was quite eye opening.

However, when I was thirty-five years old, I experienced a very desperate time in my life. I had been with American Airlines for sixteen years and had climbed about as high as I wanted to climb on the corporate ladder. I realized that I was not willing to do what you had to do to go any higher. I was still young and I knew I wanted something different out of life. I wanted more. I wanted more time, more freedom, more money, and more vacations! I wanted to be able to pursue my dreams and passions. I wanted a great life!

I took a chance and went part-time with American and started selling real estate on the side. I thought selling real estate was something that would allow me to be my own boss and give me the opportunity to make more money. However, I soon found myself backed into a pretty serious corner financially. My wife was a stay-at-home mom and we had three girls at home, a house, and two car payments. We weren't making it financially and I felt absolutely terrible about it.

I struggled with depression and it was absolutely the lowest point of my life. Not only was I struggling to pay the bills, it even got to the point that one of our dear friends took me to the grocery store one day and bought us hundreds of dollars worth of groceries to help us get through this difficult time. It was very humbling.

Thankfully we had God, family, and friends who helped us through this time. I also have to mention that my wife, Diane, was amazing during this time. She stayed beside me, loved me, and let me know how much she believed in me. I write this with tears in my eyes... Thank you, My Love.

This time was a major changing point in my life and our marriage became incredibly strong. I hope that many spouses reading this will take on that role of support. I can't imagine what would have happened or where I would be today if my wife had not supported me in that way. What if she would have just been angry and blamed me for getting us into a bad financial position? What if she would've been verbally abusive and called me a loser? Many marriages end in divorce over this very issue. I am thankful to have married such a great woman who was willing to walk through this difficult time with me and come out on the other side stronger and healthier.

It was not long after this time that I would be introduced to a business that would change our lives and our financial future. I ended up experiencing total financial freedom and became a Residual Millionaire. However, it didn't come without challenges and obstacles.

So many people in today's world give up on life, themselves, and their dreams too soon. When things get tough and obstacles arise, they choose to quit rather than pushing through to success. In many cases, adversity precedes opportunity. So, it's important to maintain a positive attitude, keep things in perspective, and push through tough times to your success! Don't let adversity or failure take you out of the game or make you settle for a life of mediocrity and unrealized dreams.

MY NETWORK MARKETING STORY

When I first got involved in network marketing, I was 27 years old. At the time, I was still working for American Airlines. My brother, Stan, who was seven years older than me, was an executive with Delta Airlines. He was someone that I had and still have a lot of respect for. He called me one day and said, "I want you to come to a business presentation with me tonight."

47

He had never done that before and I actually remember being very excited that he had even invited me. He said he would pick me up at 6 pm and we would drive down to Ft. Worth, TX for the 7 pm presentation. Because of my respect for my brother, I didn't even ask any questions.

On the way down to the meeting, he said, "I don't know who is doing this presentation tonight and I don't know who else is going to be in the room, but I don't want you to pay attention to any of that. All I want you to do is look at the numbers and tell me if they make sense to you. If so, let's build a business together." It's a good thing he said that because it was absolutely the worst presentation that I had ever seen and it was also a pretty rough crowd! However, I paid attention to the numbers and the business did make sense to me. I remember being extremely excited and thinking, "This is going to be easy."

I signed up on the spot and I told my brother, "I am going to kill this business, I will sign up ten people this week." I immediately thought of ten people who I just knew would sign up with me.

On the way home I called one of my buddies who was an air traffic controller at D/FW Airport. I knew he and his wife stayed up late and I said, "Put a pot of coffee on, I have to stop by and show you something." I went into their house to the kitchen table, threw down the box I had been given at the meeting and said, "Look through this information and tell me why this won't work." That was my presentation! I didn't know anything else.

After two hours of going through the information in the box, my friends signed up. Through this process, they also trained me! They would ask me, "How's this work?" I would say, "I don't know." So we would look through the information and find the answer. Then they would say, "How's this work?" I would respond, "I don't know." Then we would do some more research. It was a great learning experience and I got a new associate on my first night! In hindsight, maybe I should've played dumb for a longer period of time at the start of my business! Anyway, I was off to the races.

I called my brother on the way home. It was 11:30 pm and I knew he would be asleep because he had to get up and go to work early the next morning. I woke him up and said, "I told you I was going to kill this business. I haven't even been home yet and I already have my first associate." I was very young and "cocky."

Six months later I signed up my second associate! Now, I have to tell you, it was a tough six months. The first person I sponsored, the air traffic controller, was building his team like crazy. Within the first six months, he had eighty-nine people on his team, but I had only personally sponsored one. You only needed twelve people on your team to promote to the first leadership position, three of whom had to be personally sponsored by you. So, even though I had ninety people on my team, I couldn't promote, because I had only sponsored one. When people would ask me how my business was going, I would respond, "Great, I have ninety people working for me!" But it was actually killing me. It wasn't for lack of effort on my part. I was trying to sponsor people and build my team, but having no personal success. It was extremely frustrating.

I remember one week we were having a very special meeting. One of the top money earners in the company was coming to our city. I decided that this was going to be MY week. I personally invited thirty people to come to this meeting. Fifteen of them said they would come. I was so serious about it, I grabbed them by the shirt and said, "Don't tell me you are going to be there and not show up."

I almost wanted to make them sign in blood that they would be there. I was not kidding… I had had enough and was tired of people saying one thing and doing another. Even after that, I still had fifteen people who said, "Steve, I will be there."

I was so excited, I got there early and I was dressed like I came off the cover of GQ. I remember even counting in my head how much money I was going to make that night. When the top money earner arrived, I went right up to him and said, "This is my night. I have fifteen personal guests coming to the meeting tonight." I'll never forget the look on his face. He looked down at me and I could tell he felt sorry for me. He said, "Steve, don't get upset if all of them don't come." I said, "No, you don't understand, I grabbed these people by the shirt and almost threatened them with their lives if they didn't show up. Even after that, these fifteen people said they would be here." He just patted me on the back and once again said, "Well, just don't be upset if all of them don't come."

At 6:45 pm, none of my guests were there yet. But I was ok, the meeting didn't start until 7:00 pm. At 6:55 pm, no one. I was a little nervous at this point. That night, NONE of my fifteen guests showed up to the meeting. I was devastated. That was the night that I quit network marketing… forever! I went home to my wife and said, "That's it. I obviously can't do this business. I'm done." I resolved to just keep working my job at American Airlines. It was a huge disappointment.

The next day, as I was riding the tram into American, one of the guys who told me he would be at the meeting the night before was sitting across from me. I was just glaring at him… I think he could tell I was a little upset. He said, "Steve, I really wanted to be at that meeting last night, but we had something come up. Can you come to my house tonight and show my wife and me the business?" I had to ponder that. I was thinking, "I'm not in the business anymore, I quit." But something just came out of my mouth. I said, "Absolutely." I was back in!

I went to their house that night and showed them the business. They signed up on the spot. The next day, I was at work and another one of the fifteen no-shows came up to me and said, "I really wanted to make it to the meeting the other night, but I got tied up. Can you still show me the business?" I said, "Absolutely!" I sponsored him as well and I was finally promoted to the first leadership position in the company. This seemed to break the ice in my business and I started building tremendous momentum. I actually ended up making hundreds of thousands of dollars per year and made it into the Top 100 Money Earners in the company. It's a good thing I didn't quit forever!

That company eventually ended in an unfortunate manner, but it was a great learning experience for me. I learned, most importantly, that I could build a successful network marketing business. I also learned that I loved the business. My wife was pregnant at the time with our third daughter, Meagan, and I was on a leave of absence from American. We knew Diane was going to require a C-section, so I went back to work at American to get my insurance reinstated to cover her pregnancy. It was at that time that I went back to climbing the corporate ladder at American. However, it didn't take long for me to remember why I loved network marketing and why I didn't want to continue climbing the corporate ladder. Soon after that I was presented with the opportunity that would ultimately change my life.

A friend of mine, someone who I had known for over ten years and had a lot of respect for, called me and introduced me to an incredible way that we could get paid residual income through network marketing. He was a VP with a major international corporation and also owned several franchises. Coming from this gentleman, I was intrigued. I knew if he was involved, there was money to be made, it was a credible company, and it was worth my time to look. When I saw the presentation, it made a lot of sense to me and I knew it would work. I knew the company was going to launch in early 2005. However, what I didn't know was that I was going to be laid off from American Airlines the Wednesday before Christmas in 2004. My wife was a stay-at-home mom and busy with our three girls. I received a small severance package from American,

51

but we had a house and two cars... Life! It was a very scary, stressful time around our house. However, I believed in the opportunity, the founders of the company, the industry, and the compensation plan. I was once again excited.

My wife, however, was the opposite of excited. She was not a huge fan of network marketing and just wanted me to get a job. But I asked her to give me a chance to run with this business. I think she could see the belief in my eyes. She knew the type of person I was and that I wasn't going to let my kids go hungry. I told her, "If we get to the point that we are not making it financially, I will do what I have to do to take care of our family." Because of my severance package, I didn't have to worry about money right away and was able to start full-time in my new network marketing business. I took a chance.

I tell you that story so you will understand how I started my business. It had to work for me! I was backed into a corner and I came out swinging! I went on to make millions of dollars with this company and became one of the highest paid individuals in the entire network marketing industry. I now travel around the country teaching people, "If you are not in that situation and your business doesn't have to work for you, like it had to work for me... PRETEND!" Pretend it has to work for you! Put your head down and go to work. Start building a team. Start building a business. Start building your residual income. Start on your Residual Millionaire Path to freedom.

Residual Millionaire
Action Steps

What's your story? Your story is what will connect you with people and your audience. Have you learned from your failures and pressed on to success or are you allowing past failures to keep you down?

1. First of all, sit down and evaluate where you are. Are you moving in the right direction or are you stuck?

2. Write out your story and be detailed, including failures and successes.

3. Learn to share your story in a way that gives others hope! Your story makes you real. People remember stories more than strategies.

THE FIGHT FOR FREEDOM

> **In life, there are still some things worth fighting for, and some things worth dying for. Freedom is one of those.**
> *-General Norman Swartzkopf*

I love that quote by Norman Swartzkopf. *There is no such thing as freedom that is free and there is no freedom that comes without a fight!* I want to thank all of you who have served in our military to give us the freedoms that we enjoy in the United States. They can easily be taken for granted. I think all of us are guilty of that to a certain degree. I believe it's extremely important to remind ourselves on a regular basis that many have fought and even died to give us the freedoms that we enjoy. But, here's what I know… It was worth the fight! We, as a country, had to fight. Remaining ruled by someone else was not an option. Someone had to stand up and say, "WE ARE NOT GOING TO BE RULED ANYMORE." Once you do that, you better be ready to fight because the person ruling you has a different opinion.

I want to make it more personal. Your personal time freedom and financial freedom are also worth the fight. It will be a fight. But, if you know that it is worth it, then you are willing to fight for it. As a matter of fact, you have to fight! Would you be willing to give up the freedoms that you have without a fight? No. Then why would you be willing to give up your personal time freedom and financial freedom without a fight? So many people sit back and take life as it comes. That, my friends, is not how you get freedom. Freedom is not something that comes to you. Freedom is something you have to stand up and fight for and there is only one person who will fight for your personal time freedom and financial freedom... YOU! You have to get to the point in life that you say, "I'M NOT GOING TO BE RULED ANYMORE." Once you make that statement, you better be ready to FIGHT!

Steve Reynolds

Colonel Steve Reynolds has served our country as a pilot in the United States Air Force for over 30 years. He knows what it means to fight for freedom. He was a career military officer when he was introduced to residual income through network marketing. Even though he had a very successful and demanding career, he and his wife, Michelle, began building their business on a part-time basis. This required some sacrifice as Steve was juggling a full-time career and a busy home life with three teenage kids. Being career military, Steve did not have any business or network marketing experience. However, he became a student of the network marketing business. He got off to a good start by building his business with home meetings, DVD's, and plugging his team into his company's corporate events. His team and his residual income were growing. But Steve eventually hit a wall and his business slowed. He was frustrated and discouraged and allowed his network marketing business to be put on a back burner. He eventually stopped working his business altogether. One day, he was cleaning out his car when he found an old DVD from his company. It was at that time that he realized he had given up and was reminded why he had started his network marketing business in the first place. He believed in the power of residual income and he wanted the financial freedom that it could provide. He knew it was time to fight. He had to fight for what he believed in. He had to fight for his personal freedom. He chose to change and get back to building his network marketing business and his residual income. It wasn't easy. Starting over never is! However, not long after that, he had some leaders join his team who caught the vision of what the business could do for them. This team propelled Steve to the top position in his company. He became one of the top leaders and changed his financial future. He is a great example of dusting yourself off, getting back up, and starting over. He's a great example of fighting for freedom. Today, Steve is a Residual Millionaire and he has helped many others get their businesses airborne and flying high! Thank you for your service, SIR, and thank you for your leadership.

For Michelle and I, our network marketing business has been a personal development journey with a great compensation plan attached to it! We both have learned over the years that the true reward was our personal growth. Our lives have been enriched through our network marketing business and the relationships that have been created are priceless.

-Colonel Steve Reynolds

In your fight for freedom, I think there are several core elements that have to be present in order for you to win the battle:

1. An Overwhelming Desire to Win
2. A Long-Term Commitment to Fight
3. A Singular Focus

AN OVERWHELMING DESIRE TO WIN

You have to want to win the battle so much that you are willing to do what you have to do. It has to come from deep within you. It cannot be something that you are just playing around with. That simply does not work. Those who have an overwhelming desire to win go above and beyond to be the best. They practice their skill until it becomes second nature and they know that they can compete with anyone.

There once was a young boy who grew up in North Carolina. His brother was always beating him in basketball, so he never dreamed of being an NBA player. When he entered high school, he was a typical 15-year old athlete. He was 5'10" and playing three sports, but he wasn't really crazy about any of them. In his sophomore year, something happened that would have a profound impact on him and the entire basketball world. He was refused a chance to play on the varsity team and the position was instead given to a friend of his that was 6'5".

This rejection pushed him to prove that he could play basketball as well as anyone else. He began practicing every day. The rest of the story is history. He ended up receiving a full scholarship to the University of North Carolina where he had the game-winning shot in the 1982 College Final Four

Championship against the Georgetown Hoyas. He went on to win College Player of the Year in the 1983-84 season and helped the Men's USA Basketball Team win a Gold Medal in the 1984 Olympics. He went on to become, arguably, the greatest player to ever play professional basketball, winning three Most Valuable Player Awards, seven consecutive scoring titles, and three consecutive NBA Championships with the Chicago Bulls.

His name is Michael Jordan. He had an overwhelming desire to win, and he was driven to prove that he was the best.

> **"If you accept the expectations of others, especially negative ones, then you never will change the outcome."**[2]
>
> -*Michael Jordan*

A LONG-TERM COMMITMENT TO FIGHT

It was the day after Christmas and Patrick Finney had a terrible headache. He figured he could just sleep it off, but when he woke from his nap, he couldn't even get out of bed. He couldn't move his legs. Almost immediately, his doctor recognized that something was wrong neurologically. After an MRI and multiple tests, the diagnosis came on New Year's Eve, 1998. Patrick had multiple sclerosis, a chronic neurological disease that can cause blindness, loss of balance, slurred speech, extreme fatigue and paralysis. MS is an unpredictable disease. It can cause minor symptoms in some, yet be totally disabling for others.

For Patrick, it hit hard. His doctor advised him not to

overexert himself and prescribed weekly injections. Frustrated with the process, Patrick decided to implement his own plan, a healthy diet and exercise. However, he couldn't walk! He said, "My brain was telling my legs to move, but they weren't moving. They weren't doing anything."

He said, "Neurologically, after a stroke, the pathways to the brain must be rerouted. I figured, 'Why can't that happen for me too?'" He was determined to win. After weeks of focusing on a single movement, one day he was able to get movement in his foot. He then focused on his knees and quads. Then he started on his left foot. He kept focusing and practicing small movements, and out of sheer grit and defiance of the doctor, who in 1998 told him he should not overexert himself, he taught himself how to walk.

However, what he did not know at the time was that between 1998 and 2005 he would have to retrain himself to walk nine more times. He said, "It was always like taking one step forward and two steps back." The MS would return and zap all of his energy and negate all the progress he had made.

One day, when he was struggling to walk again, he made himself a promise that if he ever walked again, he would compete in a half marathon. Seven years later, he made good on his promise in the White Rock Lake Marathon. It took him four hours to finish and he was one of the last ones to cross the finish line, but he did it!

This inspired him even more. In 2010, he took on the 50-by-50 Challenge to run a marathon in every state by the time he turned 50. He was forty-seven at the time. In September, 2011, he completed his 50th state. He became the first person with MS to complete a marathon in all fifty states and is an example to all of the power of determination and persistence. Dr. Elliot Frohman, Director of the Multiple Sclerosis Program at UT Southwestern Medical Center, says, "It is extraordinary.

Other people could take many lessons from his playbook."[3]

At the time of the writing of this book, Patrick has competed in over 100 marathons! He says, "Take the word can't out of your vocabulary. When you take it out, it gives you the opportunity to see what you can do." He's convinced that if he would have listened to his first doctor, he would have ended up in a wheel chair. Instead, he is inspiring people all over the world to do more. Ed Swiatocha, Patrick's Manager, says, "He's one of those people who can say to anybody that if I can do it, you can too. He's a hero and a role model."[4]

So many people never get to experience freedom because they are not truly committed to having it. As I mentioned earlier, freedom is something you have to fight for, but it is also a battle that you have to be committed to long-term. When you get knocked down, you have to get up, even if you have to retrain yourself to walk. Victory usually does not come overnight. So many people want to have instant success or instant freedom. They don't want to be committed to a long-term battle.

Once you decide that you don't want to be ruled anymore, once you decide that you are going to fight, once you decide that you are going to join the army of Residual Millionaires who are fighting for time freedom and financial freedom, be committed long-term! Don't quit when you encounter the inevitable disappointments, frustrations, and rejections. Some people may say you can't win this battle. Some people may say you can't play in this game. Some people may say you're not good enough to be on this team. However, if you were fighting to walk again, you would not be deterred by the daily battle or the naysayers. If you were truly committed to walking or even as in Patrick's case, running, you would be determined to overcome the obstacles and challenges. You have to have the same mindset in your fight for time freedom and financial freedom.

So many people give up over minor setbacks and disappointments. They let little things take them completely out of the battle. Be committed to the process! Be committed to the battle! Be committed to the army that you are fighting with and that is fighting with you. Don't lose heart. Don't lose hope. Don't lose focus.

A SINGULAR FOCUS

You've heard the saying, "If you chase two rabbits, you will catch neither." You have to be committed to your success and firm in your resolve. You must avoid distractions that can take you out of the game. There's a reason they put blinders on racehorses! They don't want them looking to the right or to the left and being distracted from running the race.

I want you to imagine that you are in an army. Now imagine that you are in a battle for your freedom. You are on the front lines and your army is being attacked. Shots are being fired everywhere and people around you are being killed. You are fighting for your life. Now, imagine you look over at the guy next to you and he is texting! Yes, texting on a phone! Would that make you mad?

That's what many people do on their path to financial freedom. They get distracted from the battle at hand and end up doing things that are irrelevant and things that can ultimately sabotage their entire mission. There's nothing wrong with texting, but in that situation it could get you killed! The example of texting in a war is equivalent to doing anything that distracts you from your goal of financial freedom and time freedom.

It's easy to get distracted. That's why it's important to have long-term and short-term goals that hold you accountable to your ultimate goal. In your decision-making processes, you make your decisions based on your fight for freedom. You have to ask yourself, "Does this help me reach my ultimate goal or is it just a distraction from the battle that I am fighting?"

Another key to success in your battle for freedom is having other soldiers that hold you accountable. It's hard to win a war by yourself! Imagine fighting in a war and telling your general, "I've got this. I'm just going to take off on my own. I don't really need anyone else's help. I'll catch up with you guys later." That would be absurd! The same is true in your personal fight for freedom. It takes an army to win a war. You have to build alliances and depend on the talents and help of many. One of the biggest mistakes that people make is thinking they can win this war by themselves. It is absurd.

Residual Millionaire
Action Steps

Are you fighting for your freedom? Your life is worth fighting for! Your time freedom, your financial freedom, and your purpose in life are worth fighting for!

1. Have a clear vision of your ultimate goal.
2. Get ready for battle.
3. Get armed with the skills, training, weapons, and mindset that will be needed to win the war.
4. Fight!

Do you have an overwhelming desire to win or are you wishing things were different?

1. Jim Rohn said, "Don't wish it were easier, wish you were better."
2. If you want to win, you have to be the best. Practice your skills daily so you can prove to the world you are the best.
3. Even the best lose sometimes. Don't allow temporary failures to take you completely out of the game.
4. Make a long-term commitment to fight. Put it in writing. How long will you commit to your business?

Are you FOCUSED? No, are you REALLY FOCUSED?

1. Freedom requires a laser-beam focus. Imagine holding a magnifying glass on your target until the sun shines through it and starts a fire. You can't move it before the fire is started and then come back to it. You would be starting all over again! You have to hold it in place until your target catches fire. The same is true in your fight for freedom. Focus!

2. You have to remove distractions from your life. Ask yourself, "Does this help me in my quest for freedom? Does this help me reach my ultimate goal?" If the answer is no, it either needs to be removed or put on hold for a while.

3. Set short-term goals that will force you to focus. I recommend 60-Day or 90-Day blasts. You would be amazed what you can accomplish in 60-90 days. During that 60-90 day blast, remove ALL distractions.

4. Stay away from negative people/relationships during your blast. I don't say you have to kill relationships completely, but you can kill them for 60-90 days!

5. Remember, even winners lose sometimes. Don't allow temporary failures to take you completely out of the game. Allow them to make you better. Keep honing your skills.

6. Lastly, get accountability partners that will help you stay focused and push you to do more than you ever thought you could do.

THE ART OF OVERCOMING OBJECTIONS

> **Opposition is a natural part of life. Just as we develop our physical muscles through overcoming opposition- such as lifting weights- we develop our character muscles by overcoming challenges and adversity.[1]**

-Stephen R. Covey

KNOW BEFORE YOU GO

Things aren't always as they appear. While on a family vacation at the beach, one of my daughters learned this the hard way. We had just pulled up to the hotel, unloaded all of our luggage, and were starting to head into the hotel when all of a sudden, my youngest daughter, Meagan, screamed, "Shark!" She took off running toward the hotel entrance and we didn't even know what she was talking about. But she had spotted a huge saltwater tank directly behind the check-in counter. It had three to four foot sharks swimming in it. She was running

66

full speed and couldn't wait to see them up close. What she didn't realize, and quite frankly we didn't either, was that the glass doors going into the hotel were so clean that you couldn't see them. It looked like it was an open-air entrance, but it was solid glass across the front of the hotel entrance. Needless to say, Meagan did a total face plant into the glass doors. Her sisters, of course, were literally on the ground laughing. While I was trying to comfort Meagan and get her sisters to stop laughing, all of a sudden, my wife, Diane, started giggling. Then I started laughing and ultimately even Meagan started laughing. We all had a good laugh that day and it is something that our family still laughs about today.

In our business, sometimes I hear people scream, "Money!" and then take off running in their new network marketing business without getting trained and having the proper knowledge needed to get off to a great start. Inevitably, they end up doing a face plant into the glass doors of false expectations, opposition, and objections, while all their friends and family are getting a good laugh. It's better to be trained properly and know before you go!

FEEL, FELT, FOUND

I don't like painting fairy-tale pictures and making it sound like it is easy, nothing but fun, and nothing but making lots of money. I want to be real with you about some of the negatives and challenges of building a successful network marketing business and achieving financial independence. Just like anything else in life, there are inevitable obstacles you will have to overcome.

I've always taught that if you don't become a problem-solver, you will always work for one. Successful business ownership requires problem solving, handling objections, and overcoming adversity. One of my business mentors taught me that successful people expect adversity. When it raises its ugly head, they say, "I knew you were coming and I have to find a way over, around, or through you because I am going to be successful and you are not going to stop me".

This is such an important part of success. Overcoming objections is an art. But it's an art that can be learned. When I was a customer service manager at American Airlines, I would get called out to the gate in extreme cases where, many times, customers would be irate. I learned that arguing with those customers did not end up well. I also learned that by agreeing with the customer, showing them that I truly cared, and having a calm talk with them away from the heated atmosphere, usually brought the emotions and tempers down and led to an agreed-upon resolution.

Success in overcoming objections in your network marketing business, and in life, generally has a lot to do with how you talk to people. The key here is not to argue and get in an adversarial position with them. I believe the best way to talk to them is with the Feel, Felt, Found method: "I know how you feel, I felt the same way, but here's what I found." Then share facts and credibility. Documentation beats conversation.

According to the Direct Selling Association[2]:

Despite the economic climate, direct selling continues to be a source of income and support for independent consultants across the U.S. The U.S. direct selling market grew faster than the overall U.S. economy, which grew 4 percent as measured by gross domestic product (GDP). In 2012, U.S. direct sales were more than $31 billion with nearly 16 million direct sellers nationwide, the vast majority being independent business people – micro-entrepreneurs – whose purpose is to sell the product/service of the company they voluntarily choose to represent. Global direct sales increased 5.4 percent from $158.3 billion in 2011 to $166.9 billion in 2012. The U.S. was ranked as the top direct selling market in the world with 19 percent of worldwide sales in 2012. Japan came in second with $22.7 billion (14 percent), *followed by China at $20.0 billion (12 percent), Brazil at $14.6 billion (9 percent) and South Korea at $13.3 billion (8 percent).*

This is great information to be able to share with prospects regarding the growth in the network marketing industry.

One of the biggest objections that I see in my business is the objection of time. Most people are so busy they can't even think straight. The thought of adding another thing to their plate is sometimes more than they can bear. There's no doubt in my mind that a major part of my success in network marketing was due to learning how to overcome this objection. I always let the person know that this was not about their time. I pointed to our system and showed them how it would allow them to build their business with very little personal time invested, I showed them how they could create leverage. I assured them that I would help them build their team. I learned to say, "I will do all the work and we both make money." Successful people like to hear that. Many times they would repeat it to me by saying, "Let me get this straight, you'll do all the work and we both make money?" I would say, "Yes!" Successful people understand leverage, and I explained to them how they could leverage my time and experience and I could leverage their contacts… Their network, my legwork! It's a win-win. I never tried to convince them that they had to put lots of time into their business and go to lots of meetings. I knew that if I could just get them started, introduce them to other leaders and the culture of the company, and get them making money, they would eventually fall in love with the business and the people and begin to give it more time. Many times, the successful people who told me, "I will never go to meetings or speak in front of the room," were the one's running the meeting in a matter of weeks!

Susan Fisher

Susan Fisher has a special place in my heart. She's my sister! She was a high school principal working 70-80 hours per week when I introduced her to residual income through network marketing. I honestly did not want to share the information with her because she was the busiest person that I knew. She was so busy, I figured she would just look at me and say, "Steve, I don't have time to do anything else," and I would've agreed with her! But I went to her house on a Saturday morning, knowing she would be recovering from the previous week. I shared the information with her and said, "Susan, I'm going to make a lot of money in this business with or without you, but I would rather it be with you!" Her first thought was that she didn't have time for anything else. However, she knew she had to do something. Susan had a slight heart attack in her first year as a high school principal. The stress was intense. She began working her network marketing business on a very part-time basis, in addition to her demanding high school principal job. She started her business by having home meetings on Saturdays and, during the week, leveraging my time. She invited eight people to her first home meeting to see the business plan and they all got in the business. Within two years, her little part-time network marketing business had surpassed her high school principal salary. However, this was because she was willing to make sacrifices that many people are, quite frankly, not willing to make. She was willing to spend time building a business after a long, stressful day at work. While many choose to go home and spend time in front of the television (also known as the Electronic Income Reducer), Susan chose to build a network marketing team. Because of her hard work and sacrifices, she was able to retire ten years early from education. What's ten years of your life worth? She is now one of the highest paid women in network marketing and has literally made millions of dollars. Her team has grown to over 25,000 associates. She has total time freedom and no more stress! She is a Residual Millionaire and a tremendous example of sacrificing for a while in order to get your time back. Susan, thank you for being such a great leader and such a great sister to me. Thank you for helping me become a Residual Millionaire. I love you.

> **Network Marketing saved my life, literally and financially. Retiring ten years early and being able to help others change their lives as well has been a huge blessing. My residual income has allowed me to help my parents in their retirement years and given me the time freedom to do the things I love: Travel and spending time with friends and family.**
>
> *-Susan Fisher*

You will hear many different objections…
I don't have time.
I don't have a lot of contacts.
I am not a salesperson.
I am not a good speaker.
I don't need the money.
I don't have the money.
I don't want to approach my friends.
I don't like multi-level marketing.
I don't have any friends.
I'm white, I'm black, I'm Hispanic, I'm too young, I'm too old, and the list goes on…

I overcome these by saying, "Let's find someone who does have time. Let's find someone who does have a lot of contacts and is a person of influence. Let's find someone who is a salesperson, a good speaker, needs the money, has the money, likes mlm, etc."

Learn to ask, "Who do you know? Who do you know that likes to make money? Who do you know that is a person of credibility and influence? Who do you know that is success-minded and positive? Who do you know that is entrepreneurial, business-minded, and already successful? Who do you know that has the money to get started? Who can we show the plan to so I can show you how we can build your team and start creating leverage and residual income for you?"

"IS THIS A PYRAMID?"

One of the objections that you sometimes have to deal with is the stigma associated with network marketing. Some even use the term pyramid scheme. We've all heard people say, "Is that one of those pyramid deals?" Many people have been affected by different things in their lives and some have preconceived ideas regarding network marketing. But, in my opinion, this can be overcome with a little education, kindness, understanding and sometimes even a little humor.

Many times I compare it to the real estate and insurance industries. In the real estate and insurance industries you have brokers and agents. An agent is paid only for what he sells. A broker is able to hire multiple agents and is paid a percentage or commission on what ALL of his agents sell. Brokers are able to create leverage! If one broker has 3 agents and another broker has 3,000 agents, which one makes the most money? The one who has 3,000 does because he built a team! He created more leverage.

It's also important to learn how to answer a question with a question. When someone asks me, "Is that one of those pyramid schemes or pyramid deals?" In most cases, I simply answer them with this question, "What's your definition of a pyramid scheme?" It's always fun to hear these responses: "Well uh, it's one them deals where there's someone at the top making all the money and a lot of people at the bottom who don't make any money." Really? I would then usually ask, "Where do you work?" No matter what their answer, I said, "So, you mean like that? Don't you have a boss/CEO (Maybe that's you) who makes the most and then VP's, middle managers, and then all the workers at the bottom who are getting paid the least? Believe it or not, that's how a business structure works. You just have to decide which end of that you want to be on!" Of course, I'm just having fun with them, but I always explain why network marketing is a legitimate business and not an illegal pyramid scheme. You can refer back to Chapter 3 for that explanation. I show them how network marketing can create significant residual income for other investments and I always let them know that I would not be involved with an illegal pyramid scheme.

I have also had people say to me, "Well, I just don't think it's right to make money on others." Really? First of all, why would you think such a thing? At the heart of capitalism is business and at the heart of business is making money on others. Whether it is through them buying your product or service or whether it is through their efforts in building your business as employees or independent associates really is irrelevant, isn't it? Either way, you are making money on others.

Lastly, another objection that I hear sometimes regarding network marketing is, "I don't want my friends to turn the other way when they see me coming or for them to think I am bothering them." Here's my response: "This is a very valid concern and one that is in your total control. To this day, I have very good friends and even a brother who have never joined me in my network marketing business, yet they still come over to my house for dinner all the time and our relationship is still the same. You know why? Because I do not bother them or make them feel uncomfortable! I knew that I did not need them in my business, nor did I want to make them feel uncomfortable. Once you truly learn how to build a successful network marketing business, you don't have to bug any one person because you understand you don't need any one person."

Another way to look at it is to believe and understand that you are truly changing lives. I, too, did not want my friends and family holding up the crossed fingers when they saw me coming. However, even though I did not want to bug or bother them, I also felt obligated to at least tell them about what I had my hands on, and get them in front of 100% of the information.

I didn't want them to come to me a few years down the road and say, "Why didn't you tell me about this?" I believed in our company, the opportunity, and most importantly, I believed in myself. I knew that I could help people build a business and a residual income that could be life-changing and I had to at least tell them about it. If they were not interested, I moved on and told them that I would not hound them. Many who told me no early in my business, eventually joined my team due to the success we were having. So remember, no doesn't always mean no. It usually means not right now. Don't burn bridges!

Remember to use the Feel, Felt, Found Method: "I do understand the negatives of network marketing and what causes you to feel that way. I felt the same way. But here's what I found…"

BEWARE OF STEREOTYPING

There are ALWAYS those who give whatever you are doing a bad name. This is true in ANY industry. Whether you are talking about religion, real estate, investing, the legal field, or even the medical field, you will find those who choose to do unethical things. For instance, there are church pastors who throw ethics out the window and do immoral and unethical things, but does that mean that you can stereotype all pastors and churches as bad? No.

There are people out there who do network marketing in the wrong way and drive everyone around them absolutely crazy. But isn't it true that, in most cases, those same people were driving everyone crazy before they got involved in network marketing?

Don't judge the industry based on some of the people you see participating. The one thing you have to understand about network marketing is that it takes all kinds. In other words, because of the low start-up costs and low monthly overhead, anyone can get involved with most network marketing companies. However, you can't let that taint your view of network marketing and certainly can't let it cause you to miss out on what could be **your** path to becoming a Residual Millionaire. It's actually a positive thing. When you realize that our business has no limits and that anyone can succeed, you begin to get the big picture of how powerful the opportunity really is.

As you look at some of the people who have been overwhelmingly successful and made millions of dollars, you begin to see the diversity. So, there is no mold that says you have to be like this, or look like this, have lots of money, don't have lots of money, are a sales person, are not a sales person, have a college degree, don't have a college degree, male, female, young, old, black, white, Hispanic, Asian, etc... None of that stuff matters in network marketing. That stuff matters in the corporate world. What matters in network marketing is the opportunity that you choose, your drive to succeed, and your ability to build teams and lead people.

People may or may not have "all the right stuff" when they get started, but if they have a desire to succeed, they will do what they have to do to get all the right stuff. I have been amazed as I have watched people transform themselves in this business to become incredible leaders and ultimately Residual Millionaires.

Jerry Scribner

Jerry Scribner was a sheet rock hanger when he was introduced to residual income through network marketing. Jerry used to show up at a lot of my meetings. He would always come up to me after the meeting and say, "Are you guys going out to eat anywhere tonight?" I would always say, "Absolutely." He would then say, "Can I come?" Jerry was like a sponge. He just wanted to learn as much as he could. Even though his business did not get off to a fast start, he plugged into every meeting and event that he could. I also noticed that Jerry always had a positive attitude. He became a student of network marketing and was committed to his own personal development. He did all the right things by promoting himself to the different leadership positions and making himself more attractive as a leader. Jerry's income went to over $50,000 per month. I started following this guy around. I would go up to him after the meetings and say, "Jerry, you guys going out to eat anywhere tonight? Can I come?" I was like a sponge! I just wanted to know what Jerry was doing. Today, Jerry is a Residual Millionaire and living the residual lifestyle. The student became the teacher.

> *I can't imagine where I would be today had I not been introduced to network marketing and residual income. It has truly changed my life. Now I spend my time helping others succeed and figuring out where I want to play golf!*
>
> *-Jerry Scribner*

People sometimes ask me, "What is the negative of the business?" I usually respond with, "People!" When you are dealing with people, you are going to have frustrations, disappointments, and problems. It's just a part of it. I do want to also add that when people ask me what the greatest thing is about the business, I have the same answer, "People!" Network marketing is a people business and there is nothing more rewarding than building great relationships and helping people change their lives. There are many ways to build a successful network marketing business. However, I will say, if you are only concerned with making money and are missing out on the relationships that can be built through network marketing, I believe you are missing out on one of the most valuable things you can gain from your network marketing business.

Residual Millionaire Action Steps

How do you handle objections? Do you find yourself being adversarial or are you dealing with them with a proper attitude, perspective, and a cool head?

1. As objections come, learn from them! If you don't have the answer, say, "That is a very valid point, let me get the answer for you." This will be a good education for you too!

2. Build a list of common objections you face in your business and call or email some of the top leaders in your industry and ask them how they handle the objections and what they say! You will get some great ideas through this exercise. Put them in writing. This builds your documentation!

3. Get good at asking questions when dealing with objections. Asking the right questions can many times defuse the objection.

Have you been guilty of stereotyping? I think we all have to a certain degree.

1. Remember, stereotyping can cause you to miss out on a million dollar producer. You never know what's in someone's heart. You never know what will drive someone to reach an extremely high level of success.

2. Learn to find the value that individuals bring. Get to know them on a personal level. Find out what their dreams and goals are. See if they are the real deal and if they follow their words with action and commitment.

KEYS TO A GREAT START

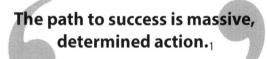

The path to success is massive, determined action.[1]

-Anthony Robbins

THE IMPORTANCE OF A GREAT START

Starting anything of significance requires extreme sacrifice and commitment. I did not get much sleep in the beginning of my business because I was busy showing the plan, working the phone, and staying up late at night to answer emails! However, I loved owning my time. I chose what to do and when to do it. I enjoyed going to places I had never been and meeting new people. I enjoyed helping others build a business and a residual income. I got off to a great start because I had to.

It's so important that you get off to a great start in your business and you help your team get off to a great start. Take massive, determined, immediate action! In the traditional business world, you hear that most businesses fail because of a lack of capital. I believe that in network marketing most businesses fail because they don't get off to a great start. I have always focused on helping new associates get in the right frame of mind to build a successful business. I would ask them, "Do you want to have a good story or a great story?" Almost always they would reply, "A great story." I would then say, "Then we need to get you off to a great start!"

When you start your business, you have a blank book and you are writing your own story. Your story is very important because it is what you will be sharing with people as you build your team. You want to have a GREAT story!

Andy Brink

Talking about getting off to a great start, Andy Brink is a great example. Andy owns Circuit Rider Ministries. He has a prison ministry in Texas and he was also a pastor and overseeing another ministry when he was introduced to residual income through network marketing. Andy simply started his business by introducing the business to a few leaders that he knew. He has an extreme story. He only worked his business for a few short months. However, what he started with a few great leaders could not be stopped. Remember, in network marketing it's not always about what you do, it's about what you start! Some people don't realize what they are starting when they start building a network marketing team. Even though he has not worked his business in over seven years, Andy has received a residual check every month because of what he started. Today he is a Residual Millionaire and his residual income has allowed him to pursue his ministry and his passion for helping people. What's your time worth? What could you get started that might pay you a long-term residual income?

"My love is ministry and helping people in need. Even though I stopped working the business after a year to pursue full-time ministry, my residual income still covers my house payment, car payments, and all my travel expenses... seven years later! It has allowed me to follow my dreams and live out my purpose. I am extremely grateful that I was introduced to a business that could provide me with that opportunity."

-Andy Brink

BUILDING YOUR CONTACT LIST

So what does massive, immediate action look like? How do you get off to a great start? I believe the most important thing to do in the beginning, after you establish your ultimate goal, is to build your contact list. Your contact list is your working capital in your network marketing business. It should be a living document. In other words, it is something that goes with you all the time and is growing.

I believe you should build a contact list of at least 100 names. Now, some people balk at that and say, "I don't know 100 people," and I would always say, "Yes you do, the average 18 year-old knows more than 200 people by first name." Some of you are much older than 18, so we just have to pull those names out of your brain!

Here's how you do that:

Take a legal pad (or an iPad!) and write down everyone that you can think of. Everyone that comes to your mind goes on this list. Here are some memory joggers to help you build your list:

- Friends
- Family
- Neighbors
- Everyone in your cell phone
- People you go to church with
- People you have gone to church with in the past
- People you work with
- People you have worked with in the past
- People you went to high school with
- People you went to college with
- People you are in clubs or organizations with
- Kids' teachers
- Kids' friends parents
- Kids' sports team parents
- People you do business with

1. Insurance Agent
2. Mechanic
3. Attorney
4. Doctor
5. Dentist
6. Real Estate Agent
7. Restaurant Owners
8. Dry Cleaners
9. Car Salesman
10. Financial Consultant
11. Banker
12. Home Depot guy!

(You get the picture... Everyone you do business with!)

You can also go through the business yellow pages to help jog your memory of people that you know and people you do business with. As you go through the A's, you see accountants, attorneys, and even the air conditioner guy. It reminds you of people that you know and helps you build your list as big as possible.

Now here's rule #1: Do not edit this list. In other words, don't think of someone and say, "I'm not going to put him on the list because he is a successful doctor. He wouldn't be interested in a network marketing business. Or, I'm not going to put her on the list because she is a high school principal working 80 hours a week. She doesn't have time and wouldn't be interested in the business. Or, I'm not going to put him on the list because he already owns a multi-million dollar business. He wouldn't be interested in starting a network marketing business. Or, I'm not going to talk to him because he doesn't make a lot of money and wouldn't have much credibility. He wouldn't be able to do this business."

Here's the point, all of the examples I just gave are now Top Earners in network marketing. You never know where someone is in life or what is going to drive them to succeed. You don't know what's in someone's heart. Give them the opportunity to change their life and financial future.

85

Jim Spargur was too busy to do anything else. He was a successful businessman and owned an automobile finance and leasing company when he was introduced to residual income through network marketing. He was so busy that he usually had a phone on each ear and one waiting on him on the desk! He will be the first to tell you that his business owned him, rather than the other way around. He was tired of the stress and the $30,000 per month overhead that weighed on him. He decided he needed to start his network marketing business and find some time to fit it in. He actually got off to a great start and promoted to the first leadership position in his company in less than thirty days. But soon after that, his leasing business really took off. He was making a serious monthly income, so he decided to put his network marketing business on hold. He said, "I just can't take my focus off of my auto leasing and finance business." However, he couldn't stop what he had started. His network marketing business took off without him and he started receiving regular checks. I used to make it a point to stop by Jim's offices because I believed he had huge potential. I always tried to be wearing shorts, flip flops, and a Tommy Bahama shirt. I would have a cup of Starbucks coffee in my hand and would sit and wait for Jim to get off of the phone. I wanted Jim to see the lifestyle and the freedom I enjoyed because of my network marketing business. When he had a second, I would say, "I'm going to play golf this afternoon, can you come?" Jim would always say, "I can't leave my business!" I would then say, "Jim, if you will just put people in front of me, I will build a residual income for you. You can do this and we can build you a business that will give you the time freedom that you deserve and want." He wanted to be free from the stress and overhead of his traditional business and he finally began putting more time into his network marketing business. He loved the residual income and the fun he was having building his network marketing business! He knew he wanted that kind of freedom all the time. In 2007, before the recession really hit Texas, he sold his traditional business. That company eventually went out of business. However, Jim became a Residual Millionaire because of his network marketing business. It's a good thing he had a Plan B! Today, he not only doesn't have three phones, he doesn't even have a desk! Jim has helped thousands of people change their lives through network marketing.

> **I'm so thankful that Steve Fisher was so persistent with me. My traditional business had me by the throat and was choking the life out of me! I absolutely LOVE the freedom that I get to enjoy because of my network marketing business. There's also no doubt in my mind that getting rid of a $30,000 per month overhead removed years of stress from my life. I love showing traditional business owners how to create residual income that can set them free!**

-Jim Spargur

QUALIFYING YOUR LIST

Once you have your list built, it's important to qualify your list. Here's what I mean by Qualifying Your List:

✓ Everyone on your list who is a person of credibility and influence should receive a check mark next to their name. A person of credibility and influence can call their contacts and say, "I've got a great financial opportunity I want you to take a look at." Their contacts will look just because that person called them. That's what credibility and influence does.

✓ Everyone on your list who is success-minded and positive should receive a check mark next to their name. Let me give you big tip here: Don't chase after negative people! Have you ever noticed that negative people attract negativity? They're like magnets. If you hang around them, it gets on you too. I've learned that you have much more fun and much more success by working with success-minded/positive people.

✓ Everyone on your list who is entrepreneurial and business-minded should receive a check mark next to their name. These are people who like to make money. They get a kick out of business and the thrill of the deal. If you know they are like that, put a check mark next to their name.

✓ Lastly, if you know they have the money to get involved with your company, put a check mark next to their name. This is important because you don't want to spend your personal time showing the business to someone only to hear them say, "I don't have the money to get started."

Qualifying your list allows you to target the right people right out of the gate. I want my new associate to get off to a great start, so I say, "Ok, first we need to talk to everyone on your list who has four check marks next to their name." I've found that the prospects who have four check marks next to their name usually see the opportunity faster than anyone. You can download the Residual Millionaire Checklist at www.ResidualMillionaire.net.

Lee Cochran

Lee Cochran built a great team by working with people who had four check marks next to their name! As a retired mortgage broker, Lee was open-minded to additional streams of income. One of his real estate brokers introduced him to residual income through network marketing. It made total sense to Lee and he had built a good name and a long list of contacts over his career. However, even though Lee had lots of time and credibility, his network marketing business didn't take off as fast as he wanted it to. It was definitely a learning curve, but he was committed to succeeding. It took him six months to get one of his top contacts to listen, but Scott Stok soon became the leader who exploded Lee's business. Scott had been an executive for several Fortune 500 companies and also a Captain in the United States Army. Lee and Scott became accountability partners and built a team together that made both of them Residual Millionaires. Today they are both committed to teaching and helping others change their lives through network marketing.

> **My wife Lisa and I joined network marketing when we realized the retirement program that we thought secured our future just wasn't going to be enough. Residual income has allowed us to not only take back control of our future, but also to improve our quality of life while helping many others to do the same!**

-Lee Cochran

89

I want my new associate to start off with positive experiences in the business, not negative ones. I don't want to meet with my new associate's "broke Uncle Harry" to try and convince him that we have a great opportunity. In most cases, "broke Uncle Harry" is broke for a reason… he's usually negative! It doesn't mean that we can't show him the opportunity later. I just don't want my new associate to start there. It's important to start with his best prospects first so he can see growth and have a positive experience. Remember, a great start is one of the keys to success.

WISE GOAL SETTING AND PROPER PLANNING

Another key to a great start is being wise about setting goals and planning. Goal setting keeps you focused on what matters. Proper planning prevents unreached goals.

What are you trying to accomplish? What is your ultimate goal? What is your dream? Where are you going? So many people don't know where they are going! **People follow those who know where they are going.** If you don't know where you are going, why should anyone follow you? Figure out what your ultimate goal is and write it down.

Jesus was speaking to a crowd of people in Luke$_2$ and said, "*Which of you, desiring to build a tower, does not first sit down and count the cost, whether he has enough to complete it? Otherwise, when he has laid a foundation and is not able to finish, all who observe it begin to laugh at him, saying, 'This man began to build and was not able to finish.'*"

In the quote above, Jesus' illustration of building a tower implies that it is a good thing to have goals, but only with proper planning and a long-term commitment to finish what you start! There's no doubt about it, wisely setting goals and properly planning leads to better results!

> *"The plans of the diligent lead to profit, but everyone who is hasty comes only to poverty."*₃
>
> *-Proverbs 21:5*

Once you have set wise goals and put a plan for success together, then it's about following that with diligent, long-term, focused action. Is this the secret to success? Well, it certainly could be a big part of it! I believe it is not only important to be committed long-term with an ultimate goal in mind, but it's also important to break that down into monthly goals, weekly goals, and daily goals.

Are you working from a daily to do list? I'm always surprised by how many people do not work from a list. I've always taught that if you are not working from a list you are not working! Those who don't do this end up drifting through life and 6 months, 12 months, or even your entire life goes by and you never reach your full potential or accomplish what you could've accomplished because you are never truly focused on what you should be doing. You are, in essence, trying to build a tower without a plan!

A daily to do list keeps you laser-beam focused on what you need to be doing every day. I recommend creating this list the night before, right before you go to bed. This allows you to wake up in the morning knowing exactly what you need to be doing and being immediately focused on it.

I don't want to spiritualize goal setting, but as a Christian, I think it's important to keep things in perspective. In our goal setting and planning, we have to remember to keep our priorities in order and infuse humility, flexibility, and wisdom.

The Bible teaches against two extremes: never setting goals and setting goals with no thought of God. James says, "Instead you ought to say, 'If it is God's will, we will live and do this or that.'"₄

91

It is good to make plans, as long as we seek God's will FIRST and leave room for Him to adjust or change our plans. His goals and plans take precedence over ours! God is in control and I don't want Him to have to remind me of that and me have to learn it the hard way!

Proverbs reminds us, "In his heart a man plans his course, but God determines his steps."[5] In other words, we can have ideas, goals, and plans, but God determines our steps. Jesus pretty well nailed it as far as goals and planning when He said, "Seek first His kingdom and His righteousness, and all these **things** will be given to you as well. Therefore do not worry about tomorrow, for tomorrow will worry about itself."[6] Our goal setting has to be done with proper priorities and right motives in mind. They should also not be accompanied by fear and worry. If our goals and plans have pure motives, proper priorities, and are set with wisdom and humility, God guides our steps to success and we can rest in that!

It is not God's desire for you to live with no motivation or planning.

We are even encouraged to study the ant and how "without having any chief, officer, or ruler, she prepares her bread in summer and gathers her food in harvest."[7]

Laziness causes a person to neglect work and miss out on windows of opportunity. Summer is the preparation time for winter and we better not waste it away! Failure to set goals and plan ahead results in "poverty" and "want."

FEAR AND DOUBT
TAKE YOU OUT

Lastly, once you have your goals set and your plan put together, it's time to get started! Fear and doubt take you out of action, action takes out doubt and fear. Jon Acuff, author of Start and Quitter, says, "Ready is a myth. Most of us don't feel ready. You have to start before you're ready. Fear only bothers you when you do something that matters. World change starts with life change. You have to get started!" [8]

So many people are paralyzed by fear. Dr. Susan Jeffers wrote a great book titled, Feel the Fear and Do It Anyway. That statement says it all. I think we all feel fear at some point, but you have to push through the fear and do it anyway! Once you get started, once you take action, your fears and doubts begin to diminish. You can then stretch yourself again by doing something that scares you. That's how you grow. If you are not doing things that scare you, you are not growing! If you stay in your comfort zone, you never experience your dream or realize your true potential.

John Maxwell says, *"No one ever got ready by waiting. You only get ready by starting. Get the knowledge you need to get off to a great start and then get started!"* [9]

93

Residual Millionaire Action Steps

Are you working from a contact list? Lists drive results!

1. Build your contact list and keep it with you . . . It is a living document.

2. Qualify your list and update it regularly with any communications or changes.

Have you been setting goals and planning in a wise and proper way? Do you know what your ultimate goal is and how you are going to get there? Are you operating with God's plans in mind?

1. Put your long-term and short-term goals in writing.

2. Operate from a daily to do list in order to stay focused.

3. God's plans for you can be seen through circumstances, opportunities, mentors/counselors, the Bible, and through prayer. It is something we are supposed to seek. Be proactive in this and incorporate it into your goal setting and planning!

Do fear and self-doubt have you paralyzed?

1. Conquer your fear by getting started! Don't worry about messing up and don't let perfectionism prevent you from getting started. Practice and learn from your mistakes.

2. Be committed to your plan. Set your mind to success and go for it with everything you have.

Goals: Date:

_____ | _____

_____ | _____

_____ | _____

_____ | _____

_____ | _____

_____ | _____

_____ | _____

MASTERING THE INVITATION

Master the invitation and you master the business.

THE INVITATION

The three main causes of failure in this area:

1 Poor Inviting Skills

2 Low Credibility/Buy-in

3 One Shot Mentality

POOR INVITING SKILLS

Inviting is, without a doubt, the most important skill in our business. I've always taught that you have to get good at getting people to look. You have to get good at getting them in front of the information and you have to have a simple way of doing this. In order to do this, it's important to understand the psychology of the invitation. When you start talking to someone about an appointment to see your business opportunity, they usually immediately have ten questions to ask you. Their goal is to get enough information out of you to be able to tell you, "NO." Your goal is to get an appointment. So, you have to have a plan and keep it simple.

I start by asking a simple question like, "Do you keep your options open for additional streams of income?" I would then ask, "Do you have any residual, passive income?" Most people answer no to this question. I then ask, "If I could show you a way to create a stream of passive, residual income that you could turn and invest into other things that create more passive, residual income, would you be willing to look?" So, either way, I ultimately say, "I need less than twenty minutes of your time to show you an incredible way to create residual income. I have today at 12 pm or tomorrow morning at 8 am available, will one of those work for you?"

Remember, they have ten questions to ask. So, I want to be the one asking the questions. This does two things:

1   It puts me in control of the conversation and it gets the prospect thinking about how to answer my questions, rather than thinking of his. By offering two options, it gets them thinking about which one works for them.
2   Offering two options also lets them know that I am in control of my schedule.

With this first question, I have told him/her what I want to meet about and gone straight to setting the appointment. In many cases, they say, "I'm interested, but what is it?" I don't mind answering this question. I tell them just a little about the opportunity and give them some of the credibility of the company and the industry. I then say, "So, what works best for you, today at 12 pm or tomorrow at 8 am?" I go right back to setting the appointment.

If they start asking a second question, I kindly interrupt them and say, "John, do you know that people remember 10% of what you tell them? If I stand here and answer your questions and give you 10% of the information, that means you are going to get home with 1% of the information and you and I both know what your decision is based on 1% of the information. That's not fair to you and it's not fair to me. All I want you to do is see 100% of the information so you can make an educated decision and I respect educated decisions. John, I promise you this is worth your time. So, 12 pm today or 8 am tomorrow?"

I go right back to setting the appointment. This lets John know that I am not answering any more questions and it allows me to avoid the Valley of Death, which is simply answering questions and giving bits and pieces of the information. It's called the Valley of Death for a reason… you die there!

If you master the invitation, you master the business. Poor inviting skills can push your prospects away and cause you to fail. But if you master the invitation, it can make you millions.

LEARN TO BRIDGE
The Valley of Death

invitation

presentation

←**ON THE LEFT,**
you have the invitation.

ON THE RIGHT,➤
you have the presentation.

The key is to **NOT** mix
the invitation with the
business presentation!

Get good at bridging over the
valley of death and you will have
much more success in
building your team!

Terri Hatch

Terri Hatch became a master at introducing people to the business and getting them in front of leaders. Terri was a sales representative for a very large company when she was introduced to residual income through network marketing. She also had a daughter who had a medical condition that required over $1,000 per month in medical bills and prescriptions. Terri thought, "If I could just create enough to cover our medical bills, that would be a tremendous blessing." So she started working on her Plan B. However, she was scared to death of speaking in front of crowds. She was committed to plugging into her company's meetings and corporate events and taking guests with her! Even though she has never done a presentation in front of a crowd, she is one of the highest paid individuals in network marketing. She simply got good at getting people to look and became a master recruiter. Today, her team is over 10,000 strong and she is a Residual Millionaire. She far surpassed being able to cover her daughter's monthly medical bills! Interestingly, Terri was laid off from her job in 2009, five weeks before her 25th anniversary with the company. Her husband, Bryan, was laid off three months later, but because they had built a Plan B that surpassed both of their Plan A's, they were able to transition to full-time in their network marketing business without the stress and financial pressure that most people face after being laid off.

> *I am so thankful and grateful for our network marketing business. In hindsight, it was the smartest thing we have ever done! It has been a lifesaver for us in so many ways. The relationships, the residual income, and the time freedom are just priceless.*

-*Terri Hatch*

LOW CREDIBILITY/BUY-IN

Low Credibility/Buy-in is also a major obstacle to mastering the invitation and building a team. If someone has great inviting skills but doesn't have credibility with or buy-in from the person they want to recruit, the prospect may like what they see, but decide not to get involved because of a lack of confidence in the person sharing it with them.

John Maxwell, in his book The 21 Irrefutable Laws of Leadership, said, "We buy into the leader before we buy into the vision."

The good news is that low credibility/buy-in is something that you can fix. There are several ways to fix your credibility/buy-in:

1. Having a long-term commitment.
   As you stick with something and push through to success your credibility increases!
2. Another way you fix your credibility is personal development.
   You have to be committed to this daily process. As you make yourself better and more attractive, your credibility/buy-in grows.
3. You also fix your credibility by operating with integrity at all times.
   What a novel idea!
4. Lastly, you fix your credibility by hanging around credible people and leaders who push you to be better and become more.
   Hanging around the right leaders inspires you, keeps you accountable, and raises your credibility by association.

ONE-SHOT MENTALITY

The third obstacle to success in the invitation is the one-shot mentality. This is the belief that you can just "hit" one person who explodes your business and then you can retire on an island somewhere and just sit back and cash your residual checks. It's a lazy approach to the business and success. Many new associates come into the business with this mindset, but the leaders in this business don't approach it that way. Residual Millionaires realize that success is a process that takes time. They understand that true success is about developing lots of great leaders and helping lots of people, not just getting lucky and finding one. They have a long-term commitment to success, not a one-shot mentality or a desire to sit on easy street and do nothing.

CIRCLE OF INFLUENCE

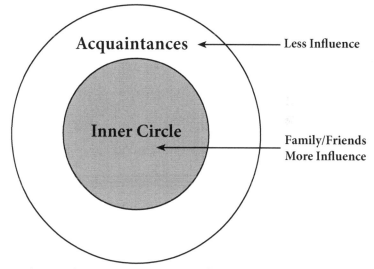

This is what we call the Circle of Influence. As new associates get started in the business, they usually start with their inner circle of close friends and family. This is the group of people you have the most credibility and influence with.

Acquaintances are those who are outside of that inner circle. This is where most of your contacts are. As you move from friends and family to acquaintances, your influence, credibility, and buy-in diminish. No matter how big your circle of influence is, most of the people you know are acquaintances. That means that ultimately most of the people you present your opportunity to will be acquaintances or people that you don't know and people you have less credibility with.

Let's take a look at how the three causes of failure can combine to kill a new associate's business. New associates start by approaching their closer friends and family first, which is the right thing to do. However, if the new associates don't learn proper inviting skills, they fail to even get their friend or family member in front of 100% of the information.

Since most new associates have a one-shot mentality, they start sharing this information in bits and pieces, usually over the phone and usually very timidly and cautiously because they are not 100% sold themselves. (They are not IN). They are hoping to get lucky and find someone who will take off and run, and they go about it all wrong. In many cases, they ruin their best prospects right out of the gate, the ones they have the most credibility and influence with.

By the time they learn how to properly invite, they have, in many cases, burned through the prospects they have the most credibility with. This leaves them having to work much harder and talk to more people to find qualified prospects who actually get in the business and do something with it. It kills a lot of new associates in the beginning, and they never get their businesses off the ground.

Can you see why it's so important that new associates get trained properly and lean heavily on their upline leaders in the beginning of their business? Can you see why mastering the invitation is such an important part of success?

Residual Millionaire Action Steps

Could you relate to any of the three causes of failure in the invitation? Have you mastered the invitation process?

1. Learn the psychology of the invitation, common objections that are raised, and plan your responses.

2. Evaluate your credibility and the buy-in you are getting. Can you make it better? Residual Millionaires work to improve their credibility and improve themselves to improve their buy-in. Make sure you are hanging around people who are raising your credibility and not lowering it.

3. Avoid the desire to get lucky and choose to build a business instead.

FILLING THE PIPELINE

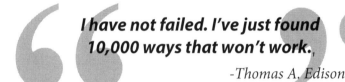

*I have not failed. I've just found
10,000 ways that won't work.*

-*Thomas A. Edison*

FILLING YOUR
PROSPECTING PIPELINE

Another key to overcoming the three causes of failure is to have a proper perspective of what it takes to succeed. Filling your pipeline is vital to your success. It is the key to getting off to a fast start and building a big team. So many people getting started in network marketing, talk to a few of their negative friends, get rejected, and then quit before they ever really get started. Then, from that point forward, tell people, "Yeah, I tried network marketing. It doesn't work." **No business would be successful with that kind of mindset or effort!**

As a 7-figure per year earner in network marketing, Jordan Adler knows about personal recruiting. In his book, *Beach Money*, he tells how he learned early on from one of his business mentors the value of filling the pipeline.

In the business of recruiting, you'll need to be prepared to recruit twenty to thirty people. It doesn't matter if you are in real estate, financial planning, insurance, or network marketing. You must recruit twenty to thirty people to start with. One third of your recruits will do absolutely nothing. One third will do a little. And one third will make a good income. Usually, one of them will build a group of thousands. In the end, some will do it and some won't. All the energy and time you put into trying to get your weaker members to grow is time wasted. You are better off using that time to help your motivated distributors and to recruit a few new people to get started in the business.

-Jordan Adler

Brian Lucia

Brian Lucia was a corporate trainer for the automobile industry and his wife, Beth, was a teacher. Brian was looking for a way to retire Beth and bring her home with their kids when his best friend, Greg McCord, introduced him to residual income through network marketing. Brian knew network marketing was the perfect fit because he wouldn't have to quit what he was currently doing. Even though he had a very demanding job and travel schedule, he started building his network marketing business on a part-time basis. His friend Greg soon began having a tremendous amount of success. Greg became a Residual Millionaire and a top money earner rather quickly. Brian, however, wasn't experiencing the same success. He didn't get off to the fastest start and while he was happy for his friend Greg, it also became very frustrating. He just could not figure out why he wasn't having the same success that Greg was having. He could have decided that it wasn't going to work for him and just quit. However, quitting was not in his DNA. He pushed through and kept consistently building his team. He personally sponsored thirty-five people and he chose to use Greg's success as inspiration, rather than letting it deflate or depress him. After five years of hard work, ups and downs, and fighting toward his ultimate goal, Brian had a breakthrough. He had someone join his team who absolutely exploded his business and his income. Today, he is a Residual Millionaire, and is one of the best trainers in the entire network marketing industry. He absolutely loves teaching others how to become Residual Millionaires through network marketing. He is also able to encourage people to push through their disappointments and stay focused on their dreams and goals because, in the end, it is worth it! He was not only able to bring his wife home to be with their two kids, he brought himself home, too! It's hard to put a price tag on that.

> *Network Marketing has allowed us a lifestyle that we previously only dreamed of. Residual income ultimately created time freedom for us because it was income that was not dependent on being somewhere punching a clock or reporting to a job. If I were still working in my previous career, my kids would barely know me because of the intense travel schedule I had to keep. I'm so thankful that we were introduced to residual income through network marketing. Now we determine our schedule and the time we get to spend together as a family has no limits. To me, that is priceless. We are so blessed to have life on our terms.*

-Brian Lucia

THIS IS WHAT I CALL THE PROSPECTING PIPELINE:

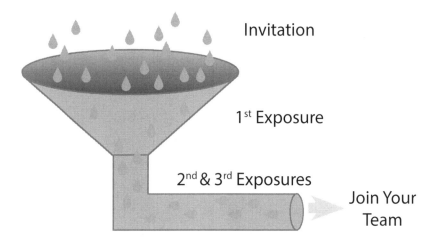

Invitation

1st Exposure

2nd & 3rd Exposures

Join Your Team

Imagine a funnel. If you put a drop of water into the funnel, will it come out on the other end of the pipeline? No, not even if you put a couple drops in. It takes many drops going into the funnel to allow water to flow and come out of the other end of the pipeline.

These drops represent prospects. The invitation gets them into the funnel. You have to fill your pipeline with people who you are introducing to your business in order to have people join your team on the other end. Putting many prospects in your pipeline produces faster and greater results. This is what massive action looks like.

You also have to have a process that allows you to properly introduce your key prospects to the information. We do that with three elements: Expose, Involve, and Edify. We want to give our prospects multiple exposures to the business and in quantities that they can digest. That way each time they see it, they understand it more. The more they understand it, the more sense it makes.

We involve them in an attractive atmosphere that doesn't threaten or pressure them. (No one wants to be pressured or pushed into something.)

We edify our system, our company, and our leaders so that we decrease the emphasis on ourselves, and create duplication. It is the secret weapon in our business.

EXPOSURE PROCESS

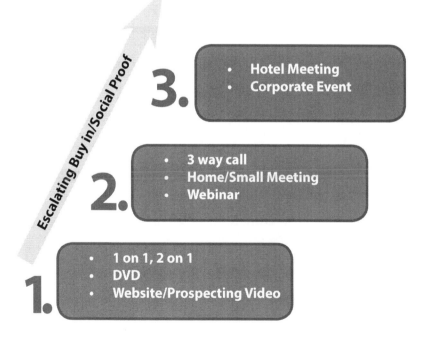

Trey Dyer

TREY Dyer was working two jobs when he was introduced to residual income through network marketing. His wife, Sally, brought home a DVD one day about an opportunity. Trey knew what kind of "opportunity" it was. This was "one of those things." He was the ultimate skeptic. As a matter of fact, when his wife, Sally, told him that she wanted to do the business, Trey really gave her a hard time. He told her he had seen "these things" before and that he was going to end up saying, "I told you so." In one last little dig on his way out the door, he told Sally, "If you make any money, you can keep it." She did. However, Sally was able to get Trey to an event to meet some of the leaders and Trey began to see the vision that this was something that could allow them to build a significant residual income. Even though they live in a town of less than 1,500 people, they have been able to build a team that numbers in the tens of thousands. Today, Trey and Sally are living their dreams. Trey no longer has any jobs. He likes to call himself a "full-time dad, part-time entrepreneur." They are able to be at all of their son Joshua's baseball games and tournaments. Can you put a price on that? Trey and Sally are now Residual Millionaires and have helped thousands of people change their lives and financial futures with network marketing.

> *After living the lifestyle residual income creates, I will never go back to trading time for money!*
>
> *-Trey Dyer*

As you expose, involve, and edify, you start building momentum. You start having success. Success breeds success. Keep your pipeline filled, teach your team how to keep their pipeline filled, and watch your business take off. Personal recruiting is the difference-maker in network marketing. It is the secret. It cures all ills in your business. It makes you forget about your problems. It gets you excited and therefore, excites your team. It keeps you sharp and moving forward. It's how you lead by example.

VISION

I am amazed at how some people never really get started. They listen to the wrong voices and choose to quit, rather than pushing through and finding a way. They never had the vision of what this business could ultimately do for them or the belief that they could actually do it. In most cases, they don't even realize what they are walking away from.

There's a biblical principle that applies to this business: "Without VISION, the people perish." In many cases, they never were really IN. I've always taught that for network marketing to work for you, you have to be IN with a capital "I" and a capital "N"... IN! If you are in with a little "i" and a little "n", then everyone you talk to knows you are not truly committed and no one wants to join someone or follow someone who is not truly committed.

You have to do whatever you can do to raise your belief level in network marketing, your company, your product, the compensation plan, and most importantly, yourself. When your belief in all of these things is through the roof, over the top, unwavering and undeniable, then and only then, will you begin to have success and momentum.

> *"VISION allows you to see freedom, ACTION allows you to EXPERIENCE it!"*

TAKING ACTION

It's true that action takes you out of doubt and doubt takes you out of action. There is a fine line here between doing what you have to do to raise your knowledge and belief level and actually getting your business started by taking action.

> *"We have a 'strategic' plan. It's called doing things."*₂
> -Herb Kelleher, founder, Southwest Airlines

I see too many people trying to know everything and "get all their ducks in a row" before they get started. In many cases, they never really get started. As Herb Kelleher so eloquently stated, you have to have a plan to do something and more importantly, you have to do something! In the beginning of your business, you have to be working on both, your knowledge and building your business. Remember, in network marketing, we don't get paid for what we do, we get paid for what we start.

To get your business started, you have to gather a few customers and sponsor some associates in your business! You want to help your new associates get off to a fast start and get traction in their business ASAP! You also want to get promoted to a leadership position in your company as quickly as possible. That gives you credibility and shows you are a leader. Create urgency to get yourself promoted. People like to follow leaders. You have to be the leader they follow. Remember, you are writing your own story and you want it to be a great one.

That's why it is so important in the beginning of your business to be able to lean heavily on your sponsor and upline leaders. Third-party credibility is huge in the beginning of a network marketing business and without it, many "Could-be Residual Millionaires" fall by the wayside. You've heard "the squeaky wheel gets the grease?" The one who calls the most, usually gets called back first! I think too many people are scared to ask for help or they think their upline is too busy for them and they don't want to bother them. In most cases, the upline leader is sitting at home wondering why no one is calling! Lean on your upline leader in the beginning. Let them know how serious you are. Let them know your goals and your commitment level. Earn their time. In other words, don't just talk, produce results. Upline leaders work with producers!

Once you have your unedited contact list built, it is time to take massive, immediate action. Don't wait for everything to be perfect, or until you understand the compensation plan, or until you know everything there is to know about network marketing. Remember, the most important thing you can do in the beginning of your business is to GET YOUR BUSINESS STARTED! The way you get your business started is picking up that phone and setting appointments to get people in front of the information. Do what you have to do to start getting checks. Keep it simple, fill your pipeline, take action, and teach duplication. I love this quote by Les Brown and I think it sums it all up:

> *"You are what you are today because of something you did or did not do."*
>
> *-Les Brown*

Residual Millionaire
Action Steps

Have you had a proper perspective of filling your pipeline? Have you been using the Exposure Process appropriately?

1. The top earners sponsor 30+ associates personally. Set your goals accordingly. If you are going to sponsor over 30 people, you are going to have to fill your pipeline with hundreds.

2. Familiarize yourself with the three elements of the exposure process and remember, "The fortune is in the follow-up."

3. Don't deviate from the exposure process. All three of these are important steps in getting buy-in and teaching duplication.

Are you "IN"?

1. Plug into all of your company's major events... Always.

2. Catch the vision of your CEO.

3. Network with the leaders of your company and even other leaders in the industry to raise your level of belief.

Are you WORKING your plan?

1. Follow the Herb Kelleher model... "Doing things!" Just make sure you are doing things that get you paid or make you better.

2. Make it a point to call your upline leader on a regular basis to stay in contact and build that relationship.

CREATING A CULTURE
THAT ROCKS

> *The measure of success is not the number of people who serve you, but the number of people you serve.*
>
> *-John Maxwell*

Webster defines culture as "The set of shared attitudes, values, goals, and practices that characterizes an institution or organization." It's ultimately what separates you from the competition. Just as corporate culture is extremely important, so is your team culture.

In network marketing, there are many different cultures that can be created, but I've narrowed it down to five key cultures that are a must for overall success:

1. A Tools Culture

2. A Third Party Culture

3. An Events Culture

4. A Competition Culture

5. A Recognition Culture

We will dissect all of these in this chapter. Your company culture and your team culture will, in many cases, determine your success. Culture is that important.

You have to begin creating leverage by building your team quickly. Success in network marketing comes from building a great team and building a great team begins with setting appointments and showing the plan. You have to have a system that creates duplication if you expect to grow a big team. Remember, the key to success in any business is simplicity. Simplicity allows you to have duplication and duplication allows you to create wealth. You should have a very simple and short way of sharing the information.

When you are showing the business plan, always be asking yourself, "Can this person I am showing the business to do what I am doing?" You will never have huge duplication if most people can't do what you are doing or won't want to do what you are doing.

CREATING A TOOLS CULTURE

By creating a Tools Culture and pointing to a system, you edify the system and it takes YOU out of the equation. It shows that you have a very duplicatable business. People ultimately buy into the system because they believe they can actually do it. You have to be "all in" with this philosophy and demand it from your team. Learn to say, "This is how we show the business."

It's important that your company has great Opportunity/ Business Presentation DVD's, websites, back-office sy stems, webinar opportunities, training programs, great company events, company recognition, and leadership that is 100% committed to the success of the field. When you have a great company behind you that provides all of these things for your team to plug into, then you have the system that allows your team to grow without you. I want my team to be building without me. My two favorite words… WITHOUT ME!

> *"Technology and business are becoming inextricably interwoven. I don't think anybody can talk meaningfully about one without talking about the other. If your business is not using technology, you will soon be out of business."* [2]
>
> *-Bill Gates*

In today's world, where everyone is extremely busy, webinars and Skype calls are also a great way to leverage your time and build your team, remotely. Webinars are simply an online presentation where people can see your computer desktop from their computer by joining an online webinar. This allows you to go through a presentation and they can hear you at the same time. Webinars are also a way to get people in front of the presentation without having to leave their home or office. It allows you to leverage your time as well.

Skype and Google+ are great tools that allow you to video chat with an individual or even a group. Your team can Skype or Google+ you into their home meetings or even their public meetings. This is the next best thing to being there. You can actually see and hear everyone in the room and they can see and hear you. You can close out the meeting and even do a question and answer session if needed.

There are many companies out there that provide platforms for you to be able to do this such as, GoToWebinar.com, GoToMeeting.com, AnyMeeting.com, Fuze.com, Skype.com, Google.com and several others. Just research the different webinar and conferencing companies and find one that works for you. Learn how to use it successfully and start plugging your team into public webinars, private webinars, or video chat sessions.

In my opinion, if you plan on being successful in network marketing and plan on being a leader, you have to learn how to use the technology that's available or you have to leverage others who know how to use it. Technology allows you to leverage your time and be much more efficient.

CREATING A THIRD PARTY CULTURE

The next part of the system is the Third Party Culture. I highly recommend you use your sponsor, your upline leader, or even other leaders in the business for third party credibility calls. Remember, it's important that you get off to a great start and that you not try to do it all on your own.

Learn to leverage leaders that will connect with your prospect. Try to match them up with someone whom they will relate to. Bob Ledbetter was a very successful high school football coach. So, if I had a coach or someone in education, I would try to use Coach Ledbetter as third party credibility. Be proactive in building these relationships so you have an arsenal of leaders that you can pull from for third party credibility!

It also makes the prospect feel special if they are getting the opportunity to talk to one of the top income earners or one of the top executives in the company. That's why building relationships with other leaders is so important in your business. When you have lots of business alliances that you can pull from at the drop of a hat, it gives you a tremendous business advantage.

Here's some advice for doing successful third party credibility calls:

1. Be sure you talk to the leader and have their permission to call them for a third party credibility call.
2. Set an appointment with the leader! Don't just call them without notice and have them on speaker-phone or three-way with your prospect.
3. Properly edify the leader to your prospect! If you have properly edified the leader, your prospect should really be interested in hearing what the leader has to say.

CREATING AN EVENTS CULTURE

These relationships are built by having an Events Culture. Events can be corporate events with your company, public business presentation or training events, or team events. I cannot adequately stress the importance of plugging into these events. By plugging into the events, you get to meet and learn from other successful leaders in the company. You build valuable relationships and what I call business alliances that are critical to your business success.

The other leaders in the company can help you by talking with your prospects at the events or even on the phone. By taking your prospects to these events, they get to see the culture of your company and realize that they are not in it alone.

It takes the help of many to be able to create momentum and more importantly, to sustain and support momentum. You will need to build many relationships and business alliances to be able to support a large organization and massive growth. These business alliances can be with people on your team, other teams, corporate employees at your company, and even leaders in other companies. They are extremely important for success. I don't know anyone who has built a successful network marketing business and a large income who did not plug into events and create lots of business alliances. Take that for what it's worth!

Don't make excuses when it comes to events. Do what you have to do to get there. If you're tight on money, find others who might want to carpool to the event, share hotel rooms, and split gas. You might even have to borrow some money to be able to go. It's that important. Events are where you catch the vision, gain belief, and ultimately explode your business.

By plugging into the events, you also get to hear different speakers. You usually learn different things from different people. You may pick up one nugget that totally changes your business. Leaders are learners! Don't ever get to the point that you think you can't learn from other leaders.

I am always open to learning. When I saw someone rising up through the ranks and building tremendous momentum in their business, one of the first things I wanted to do was get to know that person. I wanted to follow them around a little and see what they were doing differently that was playing a part in their success. I was always able to pick up different ideas that I was able to implement in my business.

It's the little differences that separate the good from the great. As Jeff Olsen says in his book Slight Edge, "It's the little daily choices that over time make the difference between those who are successful and those who aren't."

Wendell Campbell

Wendell

Campbell knows about the Slight Edge. As a Drug Enforcement Agent with the Department of Justice, not only was his full- time career demanding, it was, at times, life threatening. Wendell was traveling around the world on highly secretive and dangerous missions. During his tenure with the Department of Justice, he ultimately was promoted and became the Public Information Officer for the Department of Justice. When Wendell was introduced to residual income through network marketing, he had four kids at home, three of whom were under the age of five. Wendell started his business on a very part-time basis, on top of a demanding career and a very busy home life. I even remember a time when I was on a webinar with Wendell and he said, "You're going to have to excuse me, I have a toddler on my leg who has a bathroom emergency!" Wendell was certainly juggling life. But he was willing to make extreme sacrifices to build his new network marketing business because he saw the value of residual income. He knew that one day it would allow him to be home with his family. As he was building his network marketing business, there were many times he was traveling long hours late at night to get back home from meetings and he would have to pull off the road to sleep. He would usually look for a police station because he thought that would be a safe place to sleep in his car! He and Amy were no strangers to sacrifice. Amy walked away from a very successful IT position and a significant six-figure income to be a stay-at-home mom. For Wendell, it was not easy working a full-time job and then spending even more time away from home to build a network marketing business. But, he knew if he continued making the right daily choices and putting in the extra effort, it would pay off. He knew he wanted time freedom. His hard work and sacrifice ultimately did paid off. Today, he is a Residual Millionaire and full-time in network marketing. The time he has been able to spend at home with his young kids has been priceless. It's also important to note that up to this point, he has never been shot at while building his network marketing business!

> **My wife and I both walked away from six-figure incomes in order to be part of our children's lives when it mattered the most. Network marketing empowered us to obtain our most precious resource, time. I could not begin to place a price tag on the quantity as well as quality of time that we have been able to spend together as a family as a result of residual income. As my good friend Steve Fisher says, 'It's worth the fight! It's worth the build!'**
>
> -*Wendell Campbell*

It's the difference between water that is 211° and water that is 212°. Water at 211° is just hot, but water at 212° is boiling. It's the difference of one degree. The difference between those who are good and those who are great can be found in small daily choices and in many cases a difference of one degree.

CREATING A COMPETITION CULTURE

Creating competition on my team has been one of the most powerful things I've done. Competition is a huge motivator! Many people will fight harder to win than they will for money. Many simply just do not like to lose!

I always tried to pit leaders against each other and "talk trash" to both sides. I would always say things like, "Dude, are you going to let that girl beat you? She's absolutely rocking!" Or I would challenge different leaders to a specific contest and then bring it up on conference calls by pitting them against each other and pointing out who had the most growth. I've found that when people are involved in competition, they set much more aggressive goals and they work much harder to simply win. Let the games begin! Create that friendly competition and watch your team step up their effort.

CREATING A RECOGNITION CULTURE

You've heard the saying, "Men die for it, babies cry for it." It's true. Recognition is HUGE. Many people care more about recognition than they do about making money.

Not only is it important that your company has a great

recognition program, but you also have to establish your own team recognition program. You may be thinking, "How do I do that?" It's simple. Just remember, recognition does not necessarily mean that you have to spend a lot of money or do something fancy. It truly is the thought that counts. It's simply recognizing the efforts and abilities of your team members on a regular basis and ideally in a public manner.

Learn to make a big deal out of little things. Recognition not only makes the person you are recognizing feel good, but it also inspires others and makes them realize that they too can succeed. You'll find that recognition can be one of the biggest motivators for your team.

Be creative with your recognition. Again, make it a BIG deal. I've always found that people really appreciate seeing their name in lights, being recognized in front of crowds for their accomplishments, and being treated like a superstar. It can also be as simple as taking them to dinner or inviting them to dinner at your house. The main thing is to make it personal, that goes a long way.

Robert Bell

Robert

Bell was with the Inspector General's office of the Houston Police Department when he was introduced to residual income through network marketing. He was with the HPD for 27 years. He started building his business part-time, five hours a week. As his business grew, Robert started seeing how network marketing was a business that allowed him to help his family and friends create residual income. He realized that it was a people business that would allow him to literally help thousands of people change their lives. Robert has been persistent, consistent, and committed long-term. He's always been more concerned about the success of his team than he has with his own success and he's a master at recognition. He makes it a point to recognize the little things with his team. Today he is a Residual Millionaire and was able to retire early because of his network marketing business. He now leads a team called Residual Express and is helping people dream again and board the train of residual income through network marketing.

I came from a paramilitary structure and I was surprised by how positive and helpful everyone was in my network marketing business. I love being in control of my time and having the opportunity to earn unlimited income. Residual income is 'Happy Income' that comes in every month!

-Robert Bell

Residual Millionaire
Action Steps

Have you bought in to the Tools Culture or are you trying to do everything yourself?

1. Systems allow duplication. Remember to ask yourself, "Can this person do what I'm doing?" If your system is simple it gives you AND your prospect confidence and belief.

2. Practice using a webinar system or get someone to teach you. This tool can be used to show your business plan and also for training!

Are you maximizing the Third Party Culture? Have you been proactive in expanding your network of leaders that you can use for third party verification?

1. Build a list of leaders with their phone number and email address. Also include their titles, background, or expertise.

2. Ask them if it's ok to call them, if needed for third party verification, and assure them that you will give them advanced notice to respect their schedule.

Have you been faithful in plugging into your company events? Are you driving growth on your team by creating competition? Have you properly recognized your team for their accomplishments?

1. There's no doubt about it, events drive growth, and create excitement, vision, and belief. Be committed to not missing them. Residual Millionaires plug into events and create an Events Culture!

2. Be creative in your promotions that create team competition.

3. Be deliberate, proactive, and committed to recognizing your team. Recognition goes a LONG way and will pay extreme dividends.

BUILDING A WINNING TEAM

You don't win championships with talented players. You win championships with players who believe in themselves and believe in the program.

-Coach Bob Ledbetter

Building a successful network marketing business is about building a great team and building great relationships. Building great relationships takes quality time. I always try to spend fun time with my team and my leaders. We have team social events, golf outings, sports events, fishing excursions, etc. Mainly, I like to do what they like to do and get to know them on a personal level away from the business. It can't be all about just making money. They have to feel that they are part of something bigger than that. You want them to see that they are part of a team, a family, and a cause. It's the relationship and your team culture that will keep them in the game.

Alan

Cantrell has a very unique success story. He is no stranger to challenges, curve balls, and disappointments. Growing up in Georgia, Alan was one of the top high school baseball recruits in the nation. When he was in his senior year of high school, he was drafted by the Milwaukee Brewers to play professional baseball. Before he was to report to the Florida rookie league, he went out one night to meet with a group of friends at the local bowling alley. Before entering the building for a night of fun with friends, Alan and his friends were standing in the parking lot. A group of teenagers in a stolen car drove by shooting a semi-automatic pellet gun into the crowd. One of the pellets went into Alan's left eye and lodged next to his brain. Although Alan survived the accident, his dreams of playing major league baseball were over. After college, Alan went back to his hometown and got a job working at a local building supply company. He learned the business and eventually became a principle in one of the largest building supply companies in the state of Georgia. During the housing boom in Atlanta, his company was one of the largest privately owned employers in the state and Alan was living the American dream. He was used to making a very significant annual income. However, in 2008, it all came crashing down. The recession devastated the real estate and building supply industries in Georgia. His company went from employing 1,250 people to less than 60. Alan struggled with the fact that so many people were unemployed through no fault of their own. He had always been one who provided opportunity and helped people succeed and provide for their families. Not long after this, someone he went to church with and respected, introduced him to residual income through network marketing. He had never done network marketing before and was hesitant to get involved and attach his name to it. He was very cautious with his reputation and credibility. After he took a serious look at the business and the industry, he realized this was a way he could once again provide opportunity and help lots of people make money, while at the same time create a passive, residual income for his family that might help him get through the tough times he was experiencing. Alan had a tremendous number of contacts and a lot of credibility. He started sharing the opportunity and building his team. He plugged into the meetings and events and ultimately fell in love with the network marketing business. Today, he is a Residual Millionaire as well as a true ambassador of the network marketing profession.

> *Coming from a traditional business background, I had never done network marketing before and quite frankly, I was skeptical. However, I got involved because I saw it as a way that I could offer hope and opportunity to others in one of our country's most trying economic times. I was surprised that I not only became a Residual Millionaire, but I also became a residual billionaire in terms of relationships and personal development.*

-Alan Cantrell

135

Some people want to find ways to build their network marketing business without building relationships. I'm all for using tools that allow you to create more leverage faster. However, in my opinion, if you miss out on the relationships, you miss out on one of the greatest benefits of a successful network marketing business. I've also found that people don't easily quit on someone they have a strong relationship with.

Another way I build relationships and get to know people on a personal level is by doing home meetings. Home meetings are a very powerful way of building your team. This is when the new associate invites prospects to their home to see the business presentation. When you have a new associate join your team, ask them if they can get three to five people together at their home or office within the next 24-48 hours so you can do a private meeting or a private webinar for them to help them get their three to five people signed up immediately. This creates urgency and also helps your new associates get off to a great start, which is vitally important.

Your new associate does not have to know anything. All they have to do is get three to five people to come to their home or office to listen to a twenty-minute presentation about how to build a residual income business. You can show them an online presentation, a webinar, or a DVD. If you are not in their local area, they can Skype, Google+, or conference you in to talk to their guests.

After the presentation, answer the questions of their guests, and help them through the sign-up process. You can also get them trained immediately or push them to an online training program. Teach them how to get off to a fast start by doing the same thing. Remember, this is about duplication and in order for there to be duplication, it has to be a simple system. The key to building a successful business with home meetings is to ultimately have lots of people on your team doing home meetings without you!

When they have their three to five associates, I will encourage them to have a home meeting. I also teach them how to have a successful home meeting. I like to have five to fifteen people at the first home meeting. Each associate on the team needs to invite ten people to the home meeting. If we have three to five new associates inviting ten to twenty people to the home meeting, the team will have invited thirty to one hundred people to the home meeting and that means, in most cases, you will end up with anywhere from five to twenty people show up at the home meeting. This is a great home meeting!

DO NOT put out a big spread of food and drinks for the home meeting. This sends the wrong message to all of the guests. They think they have to be able to provide a big spread in order to successfully do the business. It's just not true. Remember, duplication is the key and everything you do must be run through the filter of whether your prospects can do what you are doing. Keep your home meetings simple and very inexpensive. The main thing you want at your home meetings is EXCITEMENT and a warm atmosphere.

The host should open up the meeting and welcome everyone to their home. They should give a brief introduction of the company and the video they are going to be showing. The main thing here is establishing credibility and letting their guests know why they are so excited.

I encourage them to then play a DVD, webinar, or online presentation. This way everyone believes they can do it. They

137

have to see that they can show the presentation the same way they just saw it. They have to believe in it and believe that they can do it.

If the upline leader is not able to actually be at the home meeting, the host should either conference in or Skype in one of their leaders for third party credibility. This also shows support and a system that anyone can follow.

The leader is able to help the new associate with credibility, answering questions and even overcoming objections. At the home meeting, you are able to have a more personal experience with the guests. It's usually a warm, non-threatening environment.

It is then about driving growth and depth on that team. As a leader, I am looking for my next leader. In many cases, they will identify themselves. They might even say they want to get a group of people together to see the information, or I may be talking to them on the phone or through Skype and recognize that they are a leader. They will be people who have credibility and influence. They are entrepreneurial, success-minded, and positive. I'm looking for leaders!

Secondary Recruiting

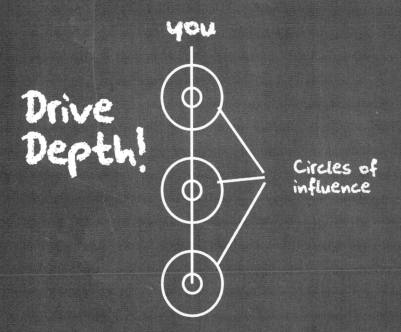

you

Drive Depth!

Circles of influence

Learn to drive depth through secondary recruiting. Leaders know leaders. Reach down and build the strength of your team by getting your leaders to introduce you to other leaders in their circle of influence. Continue to drive depth in that line with leader after leader.

Bob Ledbetter

Bob
Ledbetter is a leader. As a very successful high school football coach, his teams won THREE Texas State Championships. That is a BIG deal! He had retired and owned his own high school consulting firm when he was introduced to residual income through network marketing. As a coach, Bob had seen many opportunities, but he did not consider himself a network marketer. However, when Bob decided to get involved, he jumped in with both feet. He brought a lot of life experience and credibility to the table. When Bob asked people to look, out of respect for him, they did. He started his business by doing home meetings, one-on-ones, and plugging people into his company's events. As his team grew, he used his coaching skills to inspire them, encourage them, and to help them win. He taught his team not to quit when the going got tough. He says, "The failure is not in getting knocked down, the failure is in not getting up." Bob loves helping and coaching people and network marketing was a perfect fit for that. Just as he believed in his football players and inspired them to greatness, he believed in his network marketing team and inspired them to greatness. Today, Bob is a Residual Millionaire and is one of the highest paid individuals in network marketing. Because of their residual income, he and his wife, Sue, have been able to do things with and for their kids and grandkids that they would not have been able to do on their teacher and coach retirement. Just as they had a huge impact on

thousands of kids' lives through education, they have had an impact on thousands of lives through network marketing.

> *We simply cannot express how grateful we are that we were introduced to residual income through network marketing. It has not only made a tremendous difference in how we are living out our retirement, but it has allowed us to help thousands of others to believe in themselves and change their financial future. Sue and I love people and we love helping people. Network marketing is the perfect business for that.*
>
> *-Bob Ledbetter*

For the new associate, I want to keep things very simple. Remember, in any business, simplicity is the key to success. Simplicity allows you to have duplication and duplication allows you to create wealth. If what you are doing is not easily duplicated, your business will grow at a snail's pace. By having the system in place that allows new associates to easily show the plan, see immediate results and begin getting checks, you create an atmosphere for success. If your team is depending on you to do everything for them, then your business is automatically limited to what you can do.

Checks create excitement and in this business, excitement fuels momentum and momentum creates wealth! Duplication ultimately gets the money flowing in your organization. Many people start their network marketing businesses on a part-time basis, so it's important for them to have a simple, duplicatable system that they are able to plug into, and that they can have the confidence to plug their new associates into.

141

Willa Gipson

Willa

Gipson was a school district athletic director when she was introduced to residual income through network marketing. Even though Willa had a very busy career and two teenage kids at home who were heavily involved in sports, she saw the value of building a network marketing business on a part-time basis. As her residual income grew, she was so thankful for what it allowed her to do for and with her kids during this most important time of their lives. Even though she had success with her network marketing business, Willa continued her career as an athletic director because she absolutely loved what she did. However, this made her life busy! Since she didn't have much time to work with, she needed a system that would allow her to leverage her time and create duplication. For her, that system was her company's DVD, home meetings, and the corporate events. She leaned on her upline leaders and found time throughout her day to make phone calls to prospects. It wasn't long before Willa's team began to explode. She found a niche market with other athletic directors, coaches, and teachers. She was able to turn her part-time venture into a part-time six-figure income! Can you imagine having a part-time six-figure income? Today Willa is a Residual Millionaire and has helped many others create part-time, life-changing residual incomes. She retired from her athletic director position in 2013 and went full-time with her network marketing business. Watch out network marketing world!

142

> *As a career athletic director, I didn't fully understand network marketing and residual income. I learned network marketing is an incredible vehicle that can allow you to fully realize your goals and dreams. It's a brilliant plan that provides financial and time freedom. I'm extremely thankful that I made the choice to add this business to my already busy schedule. It changed my life.*
>
> *-Willa Gipson*

Once again, one of the great things about building a successful network marketing business is the freedom that comes with it, both financial freedom and time freedom. You don't want to create a dependent team that is sitting around waiting for you to do everything for them. You want a team of independent associates who believe in themselves, believe in the company, and believe in the system. You want them to feel comfortable showing the plan, without you!

Residual Millionaire
Action Steps

Are you using the great venue of home meetings? Imagine if you had hundreds or thousands of people on your team running home meetings at the same time!

1. Implement home meetings into your business. This is a great way to build relationships and your team!

2. Teach your team how to have successful home meetings and duplicate this through your organization.

3. Schedule some leaders to either attend or call/Skype into your home meetings as a guest. This is something you can use to build excitement for the meeting.

FINDING AND DEVELOPING LEADERS

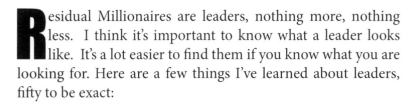

You are only as good as the leaders you are surrounded by. Finding and developing leaders is your most important task.

Residual Millionaires are leaders, nothing more, nothing less. I think it's important to know what a leader looks like. It's a lot easier to find them if you know what you are looking for. Here are a few things I've learned about leaders, fifty to be exact:

1. They have a strong work ethic.

2. They have a large sphere of influence.

3. They always operate from a platform of integrity.

4. They have a strong desire to succeed.

5. They DO NOT allow small things to keep them from BIG opportunities.

146

6. They attract other leaders.

7. They act quickly and are willing to learn as they go.

8. They are not afraid of the word NO.

9. They like people!

10. They commit long-term, understanding that it takes time to build something of significance.

11. They have their priorities in order.

12. They LEAD by example.

13. They associate with other leaders.

14. They are perpetual learners and consider their personal development a life-long commitment.

15. They believe in themselves.

16. They believe in others.

17. They like to have fun.

18. They smile and laugh a lot.

19. They love what they do.

20. They are great motivators.

21. They are willing to pour themselves into others in order to make a difference in their lives.

> *"Success in life has nothing to do with what you gain in life or accomplish for yourself... It's what you do for others."*
>
> -*Danny Thomas*

22. They are success-minded and positive.

23. They usually identify themselves, without talking about themselves. (Just a little nugget here, I've found that the ones who spout off the most about themselves, usually do the least!)

24. They are confident but NOT arrogant.

25. They are not complainers.

26. They have accountability partners.

27. They are givers.

28. They take care of themselves and their health.

29. They care about their appearance.

30. They dress for success.

31. They are busy people.

32. They have followers! An ancient proverb says,

> *"If you think you are a leader and you look behind you and no one is following you, you are simply taking a walk."*

Leaders have followers.

33. They DO NOT QUIT.

34. They DO NOT LIE.

35. They are people of their word. If they say they are going to do something, THEY DO IT. You can take it to the bank.

36. They are willing to give the glory, the recognition, and the attention to someone else.

37. They are dependable.

38. If they make a mistake, they make it right.

39. They are wise beyond their years.

40. They are not afraid to ask for help.

41. They see the job through and do not get distracted by starting lots of other projects at the same time.

42. They don't look for reasons why it won't work, but rather find ways to make it work.

43. They are competitive!

44. They practice in order to get better.

45. They don't try to re-invent the wheel, they just copy what has already been proven to work.

46. They always surround themselves with and depend on other great leaders who may be better at certain things than they are.

47. They work smarter AND harder.

48. Leaders inspire others by being themselves. People like them, therefore they want to work for them.

    "A leader is able to get people to do what he/she wants them to do because they want to do it for him/her." - *Dwight D. Eisenhower*

49. They know that getting started is just as important as getting prepared.

50. Last, but certainly not least, leaders are lovers! They love people, they love life.

This list will help you begin to understand what and who you are looking for. They are what I call Right People. One of the biggest mistakes people make in network marketing is working with the wrong people. They try to make the wrong people be the right people. This will drive you and the person you are working with absolutely crazy and ultimately will lead to failure in your business. I've found that you have much more fun and much more success by finding and working with the Right People.

In your search for Right People, this story always seems to help people get their mind around the right mentality. There's a great little breakfast diner in the Dallas/Ft. Worth area where I like to eat. There's a waitress there who has a great, bubbly personality. You can tell she loves her job. She's always talking to everyone and always seems to have a positive attitude.

One morning I was watching her go around the room filling up everyone's coffee. She would go from table to table asking, "Would you like more coffee?" As she was doing this, I noticed she never got mad at the person who didn't want coffee! She never stopped and looked at them and said, "Is there something wrong with our coffee? Do you and I have a problem? Is there something wrong with you?" No, she knew that the person just didn't want coffee. She talked to everyone the same and had fun with them, whether they wanted coffee or not.

I sat there and thought, that's our business. It's about asking the right questions and finding those people who are looking for opportunity, who like to make money, who want to create passive/residual income, who are positive/success-minded, and someone you would want to build a team with. You can't get mad if someone doesn't want residual income. It is what it is. Have fun with everyone and don't get too frustrated with the process. You are looking for the people who are looking for you.

One thing that's a sad reality but a true reality is that the people who need it the least are many times the ones who will work the business the hardest. Self-employed people and business owners, in many cases, have thicker skin than employee-minded individuals. If they don't produce, they don't eat! They usually have the ability and credibility to pull a good group together to get in front of the information. They plug in and are committed long-term. They're usually positive people and understand what it takes to be successful in building a business. They don't get frustrated easily and they don't quit.

Kirk Newsom

Kirk

Newsom is a Right Person. He graduated from Baylor Law School and had been practicing law for 30 years in his own private practice when he was introduced to residual income through network marketing. Kirk's CPA, who was a Residual Millionaire, took him to lunch one day to introduce him to a way of creating residual income. Kirk, however, was very busy with his law practice and also owned a title company. He was too busy to do anything else, but he was attracted by the opportunity of creating passive, residual income by building a network marketing team. Kirk knew lots of other leaders and he caught the vision of how he could create leverage. Even though he didn't necessarily need the income, he decided to get started on a very part-time basis. While this required extreme sacrifice and the juggling of multiple businesses, over the years his network marketing business continued to grow into a significant venture. Kirk also fell in love with the people side of the business. He loves people and he loves helping people. Today Kirk is a Residual Millionaire because of his network marketing business and he has helped thousands of people change their lives and financial future through network marketing.

> *At the height of a 30-year successful career in the private practice of law, I became conscious of the fact that I actually had very little disposable time to do things I really wanted to do outside of my career. So, my original motivation for pursuing a network marketing business was to leverage off this business model to create free time outside of my professional life. After network marketing*

delivered this end result by creating residual income whether I ever showed up at my law office or not, an unexpected health event opened my eyes to see the real reason I pursued this business. I underwent emergency open heart surgery and was out of commission for quite some time. It was during this period that I came to realize the real benefit of building a network marketing business. It was simply "peace of mind". I observed that this business actually delivered a dependable source of income that was going to show up every month either for my wife and I together, or for her alone, whether I was around or not. That brought a real sigh of relief, so to speak, and revealed true peace of mind!

-*Kirk Newsom*

"Everything rises and falls on leadership."
-*John Maxwell*

Leaders know other leaders. Those who build with leaders multiply their businesses, those who build with followers add one by one. When you find a leader, it's very important that you get them trained quickly and off to a great start. You want to stress your commitment to their success.

I always try to get leaders in front of other leaders in the company as quickly as possible. I want to introduce them to the corporate staff and the corporate culture as soon as possible. This means getting them plugged into events and making them feel and see that they are part of something bigger than they expected.

Attracting leaders starts with you. Coach Presley Swagerty is one of the highest paid individuals in the entire network marketing industry and also the author of Millionaire By Halftime. He once said something to me that was very profound and it stuck with me. He said, "Steve, most people spend their time looking for leaders, rather than becoming the leader they are trying to attract. They just need to understand, once they become the person they are looking for, they will find the person they are looking for." There's an old proverb that says,

"You don't get what you want in life, you get in life what you are."

Personal development has to be a lifestyle for you. You have to be committed to making yourself better on a daily basis. This is done by reading the right books, listening to the right audios, watching the right DVD's, and hanging out with the right people. Think, for a moment, about your five closest friends. Are they pulling you up or pulling you down? Are they causing you to be a better person or do you find yourself slipping into negative activities when you are with them?

> *"You will always live to the level of your faith. Not everyone lives on the same level of faith. As your faith rises to different levels, or your business rises, or your income rises, you will always be shifting relationships and friendships. Intimate friendships change at each level. That is part of the price of growth."*[3]
> -Edwin Louis Cole
> *The Power of Potential*

Become the leader you are trying to attract! Be committed to the process. Don't be surprised by the fact that, as you grow, your relationships may change. Embrace the relationships that make you better. Embrace the relationships that hold you accountable. Embrace the relationships that inspire, applaud, and believe in you. Be a leader, find leaders, and watch your residual income go through the roof.

> *"As we look into the next century, leaders will be those who empower others."*[4]
> -Bill Gates

Residual Millionaire
Action Steps

Are you a leader?

1. Evaluate your leadership skills. How can you improve?

2. Seek training for your weaknesses. Attend events/seminars that will take your leadership to a higher level. Be committed to continually expanding your leadership skills.

3. Do a friendship inventory. Are they pulling you up or pulling you down?

4. Seek relationships with leaders that will help you reach your ultimate goals.

RESIDUAL MILLIONAIRE
FITNESS

> *The higher your energy level, the more efficient your body. The more efficient your body, the better you feel and the more you will use your talent to produce outstanding results.*
>
> *-Anthony Robbins*

Ok, I am NOT a fitness expert and I am not in the shape Sylvester Stallone was in when he made the ROCKY movies! That's not what this chapter is about. However, I will say that your health is more important than becoming a Residual Millionaire. It doesn't do any of us any good to become Residual Millionaires and die young! So, I want to encourage you to get serious about your health. Find an expert that can help you in this area and can give you a plan to follow that best suits your needs and desires.

> *"We must all suffer one of two things: the pain of discipline or the pain of regret or disappointment."*
>
> *-Jim Rohn*

Your health can help you succeed or it can be a detriment to you in your quest for freedom. Here are some of the negative effects your health can have on your business and your success:

1. If you don't take care of yourself by exercising regularly, then you don't have the energy to build at the level it takes to create success!

2. It's hard to motivate others if you are not motivated.

3. Many people do not want to partner or team up with someone that is out of shape and doesn't have self-discipline.

4. Being out of shape affects your self-esteem, thought processes, and confidence levels, which leads to lower results.

On the reverse side, According to Barbara Russi Sarnatoro of WebMD[3], here are some of the positive effects that exercise can have on your health and your business:

1. Exercise boosts your brainpower! It increases serotonin, which makes you more productive.

2. Exercise decreases stress levels and gives you more energy via endorphin release. According to Todd A. Astorino, Assistant Professor of Kinesiology at California State University-San Marcos, "When endorphins are released into your bloodstream during exercise, you feel much more energized the rest of the day." Once you actually start working out, you'll experience less stress in every part of your life. You're not the only person who will benefit from more happiness and less stress in your life. When you're less stressed, you're less irritable! That can improve relationships with your spouse, kids, customers, and co-workers.

3. Regular exercise keeps you healthier and slows down progression of heart disease, stroke, high blood pressure, high cholesterol, type 2 diabetes, arthritis, osteoporosis and loss of muscle mass. Keep up your exercise plan and you'll find yourself with a strengthened cardiovascular system. According to Cedric Bryant, chief exercise physiologist for the American Council on Exercise, "Because exercise strengthens the muscles and joints, it is going to reduce your odds of having some of those aches and pains and problems most adults have, mostly because of the inactive lives they lead."

Here are a few things I recommend that will make a difference in your exercise routine and your health:

1. Focus on doing something everyday. We've all heard the saying, "A body in motion tends to stay in motion and a body at rest tends to stay at rest." Make it a point to do something.

2. Do cardio workouts 3-5 times per week. This burns the fat and gets you lean! Think of things that get you winded. This can be running, walking at a fast pace, hiking, biking, swimming, jumping rope, or when in doubt, set the treadmill on Incline! You would be amazed at how many more calories you burn on Incline. You can also make cardio fun with sports like racquetball, tennis, soccer, football, or basketball.

3. Do weight training 3-5 times per week. There's no doubt about it, muscle burns more calories at rest than fat! There are many different gurus out there that can give you the programs to follow that will best fit your needs and desires.

4. Watch what you eat and drink! I think these things are common sense. If you watch your portions, limit your alcohol, cut out sugar, bread, and pasta as much as possible, eat more protein, fruit and vegetables, and exercise on a regular basis, you will see a difference in your weight and how you feel!

5. Drink more water everyday. 64-128 ounces of water should be your daily goal. According to MayoClinic.com:

   "It makes up 60% of your body weight and every system in your body depends on water. Water flushes toxins out of vital organs, carries nutrients to your cells and provides a moist environment for ear, nose and throat tissues. Lack of water can lead to dehydration, a condition that occurs when you don't have enough water in your body to carry out normal functions. Even mild dehydration can drain your energy and make you tired."

These are obviously not new ideas, but I think it is good for all of us to remind ourselves of these things on a regular basis. These are not hard things to do. We can all do it! It is simply a mindset. You have to get started and be committed until it becomes a way of life for you.

We all know what it takes to be healthy, eating right and exercise. It's no secret that if you burn more calories than you take in, YOU WILL LOSE WEIGHT! There are two things involved in that, being careful how many calories you take in and actually burning calories. I don't have to teach anyone how to eat right. We all know what we are supposed to eat. We also know what we are not supposed to be eating. Even when you're eating it, you're saying to yourself, "This is SO BAD, but it's SO GOOD!"

The same applies to exercise, I don't have to teach anyone how to exercise. We all know what we are supposed to be doing. However, exercising and working out are not the easiest things to do, especially on a regular basis for an extended period of time. We are all busy and it's easy to find excuses and reasons not to. If your goal is losing weight and being healthier, exercise has to be part of your lifestyle, not something you occasionally think about. In order to be committed to it, you have to be able to see the end at the beginning. It has to be a complete lifestyle change! It's ok to cheat every now and then or skip a workout, but overall, you have to be committed. It's also not something that you can do for a week or two and expect to see incredible changes in your body, especially if you have been eating wrong and not exercising for a long period of time! So many of us want to have the value without the lifestyle change. We want the body without the work, the sacrifice, and the time.

Another important part of staying healthy is having accountability partners. Surround yourself with people that hold you accountable to your ultimate goals and dreams. Accountability partners are critical to your success, reaching your peak performance, and staying motivated. We can all do more than we think we can and accountability partners bring that out in us.

I had a good friend, Byron Montgomery, who became my workout and accountability partner. He was a Marine. That was my first mistake. We would go to the gym and he would always push me harder than I would have ever pushed myself. He was so much stronger than I was! We would be doing bench press and

Byron always added weight with each set. By the time we got to the third set, I was always running out of steam and could rarely even finish the third set. I'll never forget Byron saying, "Ok, let's add some weight and on this fourth set, this is where the magic happens." I would always say, "Byron, the magic just happened for me! I don't have anything left!" He would then say, "Sure you do, you'll be surprised. This is where it counts. This is what we are working for." I know I would have never done a fourth set had it not been for Byron.

Byron ended up having three types of cancer, but we continued working out in between his chemo treatments. I was always amazed how quickly he would bounce back. Each time, I knew I had about two weeks that I would be stronger than him. After he had major treatments, I would always "talk trash" to him. I would say, "I can't believe you're so weak!" But, I knew my time was very limited. Before long, he would be the one talking trash. Interestingly, Byron never complained. I knew he was in pain and many times he worked out in his house shoes because he couldn't get his tennis shoes on his swollen feet. It would have been ridiculous for me to ever complain to Byron.

Byron passed away in 2011, but it was only after the fight of a Marine. He inspired me to be better and do more. He reminded me about what really matters most and how short life can be. He's one of my hero's. I miss him.

Byron was also a Residual Millionaire. He was able to leave his family a residual income business that continues to pay today. What would it be worth to you to be able to leave your family a residual income business that continues to pay after you are gone?

The same philosophies of eating right and exercise also apply to business success. It doesn't happen overnight. It has to be a lifestyle change, a way of life. It's about following a plan that absolutely works and, without a doubt, produces the results you are looking for. You have to be able to see the end at the beginning. You have to see the value of doing it long-term or you will not be able to push through the tough times. You also need accountability partners who push you to do more than you think you can and hold you accountable to your goals and dreams. You can do more than you think you can in business and in life. When you think you can't go any further, push as hard as you can to go farther. The huge benefits are usually on the other side of the point that you think you can't go any farther! The huge benefits are on the other side of consistently performing daily habits for an extended period of time. John Maxwell says, "You will never change your life until you change something you do daily."

Just like with investing, you rarely see big results right away. It's a process. It's the law of compounding. When you begin investing $100 per month, it takes a while before you even get to $1,000 and even then, your growth is very small. You are putting in more than you are getting and it seems as though it is not worth it. However, as you continue to invest, you eventually get to $10,000 and you begin to see your money start working for you! You start to experience compounding and making more than you are contributing. It takes time and commitment.

In your network marketing business, just like health and investing, it takes work, sacrifice, and help through accountability partners. Over time your business begins to compound. Leverage allows you to start making more than you are personally putting in. So many people want the success without the work, the time, and the sacrifice. When it comes down to it, they are not willing to do what it takes to be successful.

> **"If something is important to you, you will find a way. If not, you will find an excuse."**
> -Unknown

161

Have you made your health one of your top priorities in life? Have you made it a lifestyle? Do you have people in your life holding you accountable and helping you stay on track? Is your health helping you succeed or holding you back?

1. Find an exercise and diet program that meets your needs and desires and that you can be 100% committed to.

2. Find accountability partners who will also be committed 100% and will push you to do more than you think you can.

3. STOP MAKING EXCUSES IN YOUR HEALTH AND YOUR BUSINESS!

RESIDUAL MILLIONAIRE
INTEGRITY

> *Leadership is a potent combination of strategy and character. But if you must be without one, be without strategy.* [1]

-General Norman Schwarzkopf

Building your business with integrity is of ultimate importance. There will always be temptations in life and in business. At the end of the day, your name can be golden, unless you taint it by operating without integrity. Without a good name, it's extremely hard to build a successful business that will last. One of the foremost principles in business and in life is that a good name should be desired more than riches and favor rather than gold and silver. [2]

> *"Better is a poor man who walks in integrity than he who is perverse in speech and is a fool."* [3]
>
> *-Proverbs 19:1*

Having integrity doesn't mean that you never make a mistake. I've made my fair share. But, it does mean that when you do make a mistake, you make it right. We are to, if possible, do all we can to be at peace with all men. [4]

Leaders work at this. They understand the importance of maintaining proper relationships and not burning bridges. They also learn from their mistakes and protect against making the same mistakes again.

I have personally dealt with several situations in my business career and life in which I had to learn some hard lessons. When it comes to business and success, I have seen some that throw caution to the wind. They have the philosophy of building their team, business, and wealth at any costs. They throw away friendships, relationships with family, and even marriages, all in the name of success. This does not make any sense and ultimately it leads to failure and a very lonely life. It is not the path to true success!

Just like any other industry, the network marketing industry can also provide you with tough, ethical decisions. You have to guard your reputation and your name. You have to make wise choices. Every decision you make has ripple effects. Err on the side of ultimate integrity and you will be rewarded in the end.

When building your network marketing business, your prospects and your team have to be able to trust that you have their best interest at heart. Trust is the glue that holds your team together. If you operate selfishly or without integrity, you will soon find yourself without a team.

> *"Trust is the foundation of leadership. To build trust, a leader must exemplify these qualities: competence, connection, and character. People will forgive occasional mistakes based on ability, especially if they can see that you're still growing as a leader. But they won't trust someone who has slips in character. In that area, even occasional lapses are lethal."* [5]
>
> -John Maxwell

One thing that really gets under my skin is when people give network marketing a bad name because of the way they operate their business. This can be done by lying, cheating, acting without morals, and many other things. One way they do this is by operating from the surprise factor. I've been told stories about people who have invited couples to their home for dinner, only to surprise them with their network marketing presentation. Others set appointments without letting the person know what they are meeting for. The surprise approach is not in the book *How To Win Friends And Influence People*!

When setting an appointment with someone to see your business, always be up front and honest about why you want to meet. It doesn't mean you have to tell them everything about your business during the invitation, but in my opinion, you should let them know why you want to meet with them. No surprises!

Another way people give network marketing a bad name is by constantly exaggerating. Some feel that they always have to stretch the truth to make an impact or to get ahead. Ultimately, this just makes you, and the company you are representing, look bad. The truth always wins out in the end. Tell the truth and work with people who tell the truth.

Other leaders in the industry and in your company also have to be able to trust you and know that you will do the right thing. If you have the attitude that you don't care what other leaders think and you think you can be a lone ranger, you have a very shallow view of the potential of this industry and the role others can play in your success.

Character is the beginning of trust. Webster defines character as "moral excellence and firmness." Leaders protect their character. In politics, some people believe that their personal life does not affect or determine the success of their political life. The same is true in business, some believe that their personal life does not affect or determine the success of their business life. However, it does. They are intertwined.

Ultimately, your integrity will raise you up, or the lack of it will destroy you. It may seem, for a while, that a person lacking integrity has success and "all this world has to offer." However, this is usually short-lived. We have all seen this play out over and over again. People who seem to have the world by the tail and success according to worldly terms fall from grace due to moral issues. This was most recently seen in the story of Lance Armstrong. It is also a biblical principle that has been proven over and over again.

"The integrity of the upright will guide them, but the falseness of the treacherous will destroy them." [6]
-Proverbs 11:3

Integrity leads to success.

In his book *The Millionaire Mind*, Thomas J. Stanley asked 733 millionaires to rank 30 factors that led to their success. The Number 1 attribute — being honest with all people —Honesty is more than taking the moral high road — it is also critical for succeeding in the business world.

Louis and Michelle Miori

Louis and Michelle Miori have an incredible story of building their business with integrity. They were introduced to residual income through network marketing by their son's football coach. Louis was a pastor at a very large church in the Houston, TX area and Michelle was a sales executive for a printing company. They simply went to the presentation as a favor to their son's football coach because he had recently visited their church and Louis didn't feel like he could say no. They had a feeling it was a network marketing presentation and they were fully prepared to say they were not interested. However, when they saw how they could create passive, residual income, they knew they had to do it. They had three kids and, therefore, three college tuitions to pay for! This "why" drove them to build their business and find ways around, through, and over the inevitable obstacles that would get in their way. You see, Louis made a commitment early in their business that he was not going to build their network marketing business through their church. He wanted to keep the two separate. So they began building their business through their contacts outside of the church. They built their business on a part-time basis, but were committed to its success. They were blown away as their team grew to over 7,000 associates. Michelle was able to quit her job and go full-time in their network marketing business and has become a sought after speaker and trainer. Today they are Residual Millionaires and not only help people in their spiritual journey, but also in their journey to financial freedom!

> *The things I love most in life are spending time with family and friends and helping people. I used to have very little time to do these things. Now, thanks to the monthly residual income our network marketing business provides, I am able to spend MOST of my time doing exactly these things! And the 'icing on the cake' is that I get to teach others how they can do the same. Network Marketing has allowed me to buy back my time while helping my family financially at the same time. Our three children are now grown and as we enter the 'empty-nester' chapter of our lives, thanks to our residual income, 'empty' is the LAST thing our nest will be as we invest our time, money and lives into helping many people be, do, and have more!*
>
> *-Michelle Miori*

The message is that you can have both. You can have success and maintain your integrity, but you have to fight to maintain your integrity just as much, if not more than you are fighting for your success. Choose to be the leader who sets the standard. Don't let your reputation be a detriment to you. Don't cave in to the peer pressure and feel that you have to compromise your integrity to get ahead.

Are you going above and beyond to maintain your good name? Are you operating your business with integrity at all times?

1. Make a commitment today that you are going to set the standard.

2. Be committed to learning the ways of integrity. I recommend a morning devotional that will get you off on the right track every morning!

3. Find accountability partners (counselors) who are 100% committed to integrity and will push you to do the right thing at all times as well.

MONEY AND SUCCESS

Money isn't the most important thing in life, but it's reasonably close to oxygen on the 'gotta have it' scale.

-Zig Ziglar

I have to say, writing this chapter made me evaluate my life, my motives, my business, my perspectives, my spiritual health, and challenged me more than I was prepared for. I am, obviously, not perfect. There are areas in my finances, my life, and my business life that I am working on as I write this book.

Let me say, first of all, I am all for making money and success. But, I also believe that it is vitally important to have a right perspective of the two as you are building your business and living your life. There has to be balance in your life if you intend to be a true success.

Those who have wrong beliefs and perceptions about money and success end up poor or at the opposite end of the spectrum, they end up consumed with acquiring both money and success at the expense of everything else in their lives.

There is no good in poverty. It is a problem. The Bible doesn't say God blesses you with poverty. There is also no blessing in having riches and, at the same time, being a failure in every other area of your life.

I've found that many people have questions about these issues. What is right? What is wrong? Quite frankly, I have personally struggled at times in understanding what is the right and wrong perspective of money and success.

Money and success can be tremendous blessings. But, they can also be something that can destroy you if you don't have proper priorities, perspectives, and balance. Just like we don't want to live in poverty, I think we also have to be careful to ensure that we don't have an unbridled pursuit of riches. You have to protect against an attitude that says, "I'm getting money and success, no matter what the costs." The Bible is very clear that this leads many men into foolish and harmful desires that ultimately end in ruin.[2]

We've all, most likely, heard the saying, "The love of money is the root of all kinds of evil."[3] Some even misquote this by saying, "Money is the root of all kinds of evil."

As I studied these subjects for myself, I learned that there are lots of warnings about riches and success and there are also lots of principles that lead to riches and success. The conclusion that I came to was that it's important to have a healthy view of, understanding of, and respect for both.

I wanted to include this chapter because I feel so many people struggle with these two subjects and have unhealthy views and beliefs, both on the poverty side and the rich side. I wanted to attack it head on. I hope this chapter helps you as much as it has helped me. I believe we all have to wrestle with these subjects individually and on a regular basis. You have to make sure you have a healthy perspective and know what is right for you.

Growing up as a preacher's kid, I heard lots of different views about money and success. As an adult, nothing has changed. I still hear lots of different views about money and success! There are thousands of books, TV shows, movies, websites, and many other sources that talk about money and success. It's in our face all the time.

As we look at these issues, I'm, once again, going to use the Bible as a reference. As I mentioned earlier in the book, whether you believe in God and the Bible or not, you can learn from the principles in this chapter. These are principles of wealth and success that have survived the test of time.

It's impossible to cover this entire subject in one chapter. I'm just going to cover a few topics:

1. The warnings about riches and success.
2. The principles that lead to riches and success.
3. The matter of the heart and your priorities.

Interestingly, Jesus himself talked more about money than heaven or hell. There are over 2,300 verses in the Bible that discuss money. That's more verses than there are on faith and prayer combined!

Do you think this might be a pretty important topic for us to have a firm grasp of? It's also important to note that you can't take one verse out of the Bible and base your whole financial perspective or beliefs about money or success on it. You have to look at the whole picture, the subject and the intent in its entirety. I have provided a reference in the back of the book that will allow you to study this subject on your own.

Once again, I certainly don't have all the answers, nor do I claim to be an expert. I'm actually far from it. I have made my fair share of financial mistakes. This is probably a good time to also say that I am not a financial advisor, planner, or counselor. I have learned a lot through my experiences, my mistakes, and my research for this book. My hope is that you will be challenged to find the truth for yourself. We better have this part of our lives right!

> *"If a person gets his attitude toward money straight, it will help straighten out almost every other area in his life."*[4]
> -Billy Graham

Of all the divorces that take place in our country, the majority can be tied to money issues. An unhealthy view of money, erring on the side of rich or poor, can lead to all sorts of problems in our lives.

> *"Motives having to do with money or sex account for 99% of the crimes that are committed in the United States, but those with money as their object outpoint sexual offenses by a ratio of four to one."*
> -David E. Neff, "Drunk On Money"
> *Christianity Today*

Many of us have beliefs and points of view about money and success that are based on our childhood, what our parents or others instilled in us, and our experiences, good or bad. It can be easy to have false perceptions and unhealthy beliefs about money and success.

So what is the right perspective of money and success? Is it wrong to be rich? Is it wrong to be poor? Is it wrong to want to be successful? Is righteousness equivalent to living a life of poverty, mediocrity, and a lack of success? If you have a successful business or career, does that mean you are chasing after riches and headed for ruin? What is the love of money and what determines that you've crossed the line? Where do you draw the lines?

So many people take verses in the Bible out of context and they don't look at the whole picture in its entirety. From all my study of money and success in scripture and other resources, my belief is that ultimately it's a matter of your heart and your priorities.

THE WARNINGS ABOUT RICHES AND SUCCESS

One of the principles that Jesus taught was "Where your treasure is, that's where your heart will be also."[5] He encouraged us NOT to "lay up treasures on earth, but rather in heaven, where moth and rust do not destroy."

What does that mean? How do you lay up treasures in heaven rather than treasures on earth?

One of the verses that is often taken out of context is the verse that says, "No one can serve two masters; for either he will hate the one and love the other, or he will hold to one and despise the other. You cannot serve God and riches."[6]

Jesus was very clear here that if your focus is on laying up treasures on earth, your HEART will be there also. The point is, which one is your MASTER, God or getting rich?

Many people take these verses and come to the conclusion that it is wrong to have a nice home, nice cars, nice clothes, etc. Some people even come to the conclusion that it's either God or money. That's not what it said and was not the point. The point was that you can't have BOTH as your Master. Your life can't be "ruled" or "consumed" by an overwhelming, unquenchable desire to get rich.

Most of us have also probably heard the verse that says, "For what will a man be profited, if he gains the whole world, and forfeits his soul? Or what will a man give in exchange for his

175

soul?"[7] It's a reminder that nothing, including gaining riches and success, is worth exchanging your soul.

We are warned not to weary ourselves to gain wealth and to even "cease from our consideration of it." The Bible says, "When you set your eyes on it, it is gone. Wealth certainly makes itself wings, like an eagle that flies toward the heavens."[8]

Instead, we are encouraged to pursue righteousness, godliness, faith, love, perseverance and gentleness. So, where do you draw the line between providing for your family, success, making money, building a business, wanting to get rich, and losing your soul? Can you be successful without losing your soul? Can you be rich without losing your soul? Can you be rich without loving money? Where's the line of loving money? Where do you draw the lines?

Several times, Jesus spoke about the parable of the sower. In this parable, He describes a man who "Hears the word, and the worries of the world, the deceitfulness of riches, and the pleasures of this life choke the word."[9] So, we have to be careful that we don't allow these things to become preeminent in our lives. Interestingly, it also says, "The one who hears the word and does it is blessed in all that he does."[10]

The message is that we don't want to hear the word and allow it to be choked out by the worries of the world, the deceitfulness of riches, and the pleasures of this life. But rather, we are to hear it and do it. This leads to you being blessed in EVERYTHING you do and every area of your life. Ultimately, it's how you become a true success.

We also have to guard against the "busyness" of life. I think we all have to deal with this. If we are so busy that our spiritual life, family life, and other areas of our life are choked to death, we are too busy and not on the path to true success.

One of the biggest warnings that God gives throughout scripture regarding riches is the warning against pride and forgetting God.[11] There seems to be a recurring pattern all throughout scripture. Here's the pattern that is often repeated:

1. Make lots of money
2. Eat good food and are satisfied
3. Built good houses and lived in them
4. Multiplied your bank account and all that you have
5. Then your heart becomes proud
6. You take credit for your success by saying, "The strength of my hand made me this wealth"
7. You forget God

As you build your business and follow the principles that lead to wealth, be sure you keep yourself in check. Be sure you maintain proper perspectives. Be sure you have a healthy respect for the warnings that are given about riches and success. Protect against an unbridled pursuit of riches. Protect against the "busyness" of life. Protect against pride and forgetting God.

THE PRINCIPLES THAT LEAD TO RICHES

Just as God gives many warnings about wealth and riches, He also talks about wealth and riches being a blessing and a by-product of following certain principles. You saw earlier that it is the "blessing of God that makes rich, and He adds no sorrow to it." There's also a verse that says, "It is God who gives you the ability to create wealth."[12]

I think it's important to note that God does not bless you with poverty. There are principles that lead to riches and blessing and others that lead to poverty. Here are a few:

1. Diligence makes rich. Negligence leads to poverty.[13]
2. Preparation leads to riches. Laziness leads to poverty.[14]
3. Labor leads to profit. Mere talk leads to poverty.[15]
4. Wisdom leads to riches. Foolishness leads to poverty.[16]
5. Generosity leads to riches, blessing, and many

friends.[17] Selfish-ambition leads to disorder and every evil thing.[18]

6. Obedience and forgiveness lead to riches and blessing.[19] Heavy drinking, overeating, and drowsiness lead to poverty.[20]

7. Tithing leads to riches, blessing and protection. Not tithing leads to a curse from God and ultimately poverty.[21]

So, we've seen the warnings about riches and wealth and we've seen the principles that lead to riches and poverty. One of the keys to maintaining a proper perspective is not only remembering God, but also remembering that He owns it all in the first place.[22]

THE MATTER OF THE HEART

There's no doubt, as you will see in the rest of this chapter and the next, God wants to bless you beyond your wildest dreams. He has the ability to bless you with wealth. We just have to pay attention to what He blesses and what He warns against. We have to make sure we are serving the right MASTER. It's a matter of your heart and your priorities.

So, you see, the lines are drawn in your heart and by your priorities. Can you be successful, have money, AND maintain a right relationship with God? Yes, but you have to guard your heart. You have to maintain a proper perspective of why on earth you are here on this earth. You also have to know and understand from whom your blessings and success come from, why you are being blessed, and what is expected from you as you are blessed.

We are told to, "Instruct those who are rich in this present world not to be conceited or to fix their hope on the uncertainty of riches, but on God, who richly supplies us with all things to enjoy. Instruct them to do good, to be rich in good works, to be generous and ready to share, storing up for themselves the treasure of a good foundation for the future, so that they may

178

take hold of that which is life indeed."[23]

It can be easy to allow riches to go to your head. One of the best ways to prevent that is to hold your money loosely and be generous, ready to share, and to give back by helping others! Give your time, your knowledge, your experience, your talents, your influence, and your resources to help others.

God is a God of balance. All throughout scripture, there is balance. As with everything else in life, there also has to be balance regarding the teachings of money and success. My brother, Scott Fisher, who is Pastor of Metroplex Chapel in the Dallas/Ft. Worth area, has a good definition of Biblical prosperity: "To live in a state of material, physical, emotional, and spiritual health." When one of those is out of whack and unhealthy, it affects the other areas.

I want to end the chapter with these thoughts: Proverbs says, "Riches do not profit in the day of wrath, but righteousness delivers from death. He who trusts in riches will fall, but the righteous will flourish like the green leaf."[24]

What a great promise and at the same time a strong warning! Our focus should be on righteousness, NOT riches. It doesn't mean riches are wrong, it just means if you are trusting in them and your priorities are not in order, you will fall. Riches without righteousness lead to ruin.

> *"The key to a right use of money and possessions is a right perspective - an eternal perspective. The everyday choices I make regarding money and possessions are of eternal consequence."*
>
> *-Randy Alcorn*
> *Money, Possessions and Eternity*

Residual Millionaire
Action Steps

Do you have your priorities in order when it comes to money and success? Are you listening to the warnings about money and success? Are you following the principles that lead to money and success? Are you guarding your heart?

1. It can be easy for all of us to get focused on something without realizing we are consumed with it. It's imperative that we remind ourselves of what is important in life and that we always maintain a proper perspective of money and success.

2. I encourage you to make a list of the things that are important to you, the warnings about money and success, and the principles that lead to riches. Put this list in a place where it will be a regular reminder for you.

3. Proverbs 4:23 says, "Guard your heart more than anything else because the source of your life flows from it." Make a commitment from this point forward to guard your heart with diligence.

DECIDE TO DREAM

> *Some men 'happen' to influence while others 'determine' to. This is the difference between followers and leaders. Mediocre men settle for good, which is often the enemy of best.*
>
> *-Dr. Edwin Louis Cole*
> *Founder of the Christian Men's Network*
> *Author of Power of Potential,*
> *Maximized Manhood*

Leaders determine to influence, decide to dream, and refuse to settle for good. So many people have stopped dreaming! This goes back to the fact that so many people don't believe that they were created to succeed. When people don't believe in themselves, their dreams are non-existent.

Dreaming is a decision. Every significant accomplishment is born of a dream. Dreamers change the world! Dreamers affect people's lives for the good. Dreamers live life on purpose and understand that there is more to life than survival, mediocrity, and selfish ambition.

Dreams are of God. All throughout scripture, God uses dreams and visions to communicate and inspire. I don't believe there is any other story in the Bible which portrays that better than the story of Joseph. Most of us have probably heard or read the story at some point in our lives.

I want to encourage you to read that story on your own. It is found in its entirety in Genesis, chapters 37-50. I'm going to paraphrase for the sake of not putting all fourteen chapters into this book. We can all learn so much about money, success, dreams, and God's favor from the story of Joseph. It's important that we apply these lessons to our lives and businesses.

When Joseph was seventeen years old, he had a dream. In his dream, he and his brothers were in the field binding up stalks of wheat. Joseph's stalk stood up and his brothers' stalks gathered around and bowed down to Joseph's.

He actually shared his dream with his brothers. His brothers already hated him because his father, Jacob, loved him more than the rest of them. Apparently, they didn't take too kindly to this dream either. They said, "Do you really think that you are going to rule over us?"[1]

His brothers conspired together, threw him in a pit, and ultimately sold him to some traders passing by on their way to Egypt. They put blood on his coat, gave it to their dad and told him they had found it in the field, leaving him assuming that Joseph had been killed by a wild animal.

Joseph was sold to an Egyptian officer of Pharaoh named Potiphar. Interestingly, in Gen. 39:2-3, it says, "And God was with Joseph, so he became a successful man."[2] It also says that his master saw that "God was with him and how God caused all that he did to prosper."

Joseph found favor with Potiphar and he put Joseph in charge of all that he owned. It goes on to say that, because of Joseph, God blessed everything in Potiphar's house and in his fields. Isn't it interesting that Potiphar was blessed too, simply because he had hired Joseph, a man of integrity?

Verse 6 says that Joseph was handsome in form and appearance. It wasn't very long before his master's wife "looked with desire at Joseph"[3] and tried to seduce him. Joseph refused.

Multiple times she approached Joseph to seduce him and one day she grabbed him and he literally ran out of his clothes and left her there, holding his clothes! She then told her husband a lie and framed Joseph by saying that he had come in to seduce her.

Potiphar was furious and had Joseph thrown in prison. Interestingly, Joseph was given favor in the sight of the chief jailer. And the chief jailer put Joseph in charge of everything. He too recognized that "God was with him and whatever he did, God made to prosper."[4]

Some of Pharaoh's servants who were in prison with Joseph had dreams and God gave Joseph the ability to interpret their dreams for them. Joseph told one of the servants, the one who was going to live, to remember him when things went well with him and asked him to mention him to Pharaoh, and get him out of prison. Then Joseph's interpretation of the men's dreams came to pass.

Two years later (think about all that Joseph had been through up to this point), Pharaoh had a dream and no one could interpret it. His servant told him about Joseph and how when he was in prison, Joseph interpreted dreams correctly. Pharaoh summoned Joseph and Joseph interpreted Pharoah's dream for him.

Pharaoh also recognized Joseph's wisdom and that God was with him. He ended up putting him in charge of all of Egypt. Are you starting to see a pattern here? Interestingly, Joseph was thirty years old when all this happened. Only thirteen years had passed from the time he had his dream.

Joseph had correctly interpreted Pharaoh's dream that there would be seven years of abundance followed by seven years of famine. He wisely stored food in all the cities during the years of abundance to protect the people from the famine. There was so much grain, the Egyptians stopped measuring because it was "like the sand of the sea."

The famine was so severe that it was spread all over the

earth. During the famine, people came from all over the world to buy food from Joseph, including Joseph's long-lost brothers.

It's amazing how this story ends. Joseph forgives his brothers and is reunited with his entire family. The entire family was taken care of by Joseph and Pharaoh. They were given the best of Egypt. They were also protected from the famine due to Joseph's preparation, God's favor on him, and because of Joseph's dream.

Joseph continued selling grain through the famine. When people didn't have money to buy food, he accepted livestock in exchange. When they ran out of livestock, the next year Joseph traded food for their land. All the money, the livestock, and the land then belonged to Pharaoh. He gave the people seed to plant and in exchange they had to give Pharaoh a fifth at harvest. Pharaoh was blessed because of Joseph and the people of Egypt told Joseph that he had saved their lives.

LESSONS LEARNED FROM THE STORY OF JOSEPH

What an incredible story of a dreamer. What an incredible story of adversity. What an incredible story of forgiveness! What an incredible story of God's provision, God's favor, and God's principles.

Here are some lessons that can be learned from the story of Joseph:

- Dreamers are not afraid to share their dream. However, be ready, as in the story of Joseph, when you share your dreams, expect to be faced with opposition, adversity, naysayers, ridicule, and even sabotage.
- Dreamers are motivated to become as they see themselves in their dream.
- Dreamers are seekers of wisdom. Joseph had wisdom. He not only sought what was right, but he practiced what was right.

> *"How blessed is the man who finds wisdom, and the man who gains understanding. For its profit is better than the profit of silver and its gain than fine gold. She is more precious than jewels and nothing you desire compares with her. Long life is in her right hand and in her left hand are riches and honor."*
>
> *-Proverbs 3:13-16*

This is not the wisdom that is known by academia, but rather the wisdom that comes from God. The great news is that God gives wisdom. James 1:5 says, "If any of you lacks wisdom, ask God, who gives to all men generously, and it will be given to him."

Wisdom leads to favor. Joseph had favor with God and men. Throughout his life, everywhere he went he had the favor of God and men. How do you get favor with God and men?

> *"Do not forget my teaching, but let your heart keep my commandments; For length of days and years of life, and peace they will add to you. Do not let kindness and truth leave you; bind them around your neck, write them on the tablet of your heart, so you will find favor in the sight of God and man."*
>
> *-Proverbs 3:1-4*

• Dreamers keep kindness and truth (integrity) with them and therefore find favor in the sight of God and man.

185

Interestingly, on every dollar bill and on the Great Seal of the United Sates you see the words, "In God We Trust." On the seal, you see the Latin words ANNUIT COEPTIS, which is translated by the U.S. State Department$_8$, the U.S. Mint$_9$, and the U.S. Treasury$_{10}$ as "God has favored our undertaking." It was Benjamin Franklin's belief that one man couldn't do it alone, but a group of men, with the help of God, could do anything.

- Dreamers are exalted to positions of leadership. Everywhere they go, the favor, the wisdom, and the blessing is recognized. It doesn't matter if they are in prison or the house of Pharaoh.
- Dreamers overcome adversity. Trials and tribulation follow dreams. Your dream will be tested. There will be temptations, attacks, unfairness, and overwhelming situations that seem insurmountable at the time. Life is not fair. But dreamers don't get taken out of the game by their current situation. Instead, they realize they are part of a higher purpose and they press on.
- Dreamers continue to believe in their dream.

Joseph had multiple opportunities to fall. He had multiple opportunities to get angry at God and question why all of this was happening to him. He could have become bitter, angry, disillusioned, and blamed his situations on everything that had happened in his life. But instead, he chose to keep a positive attitude no matter what happened to him. He remained faithful and was a blessing everywhere he went, even in prison.

- Dreamers are faithful, responsible, and dependable. They don't spend time giving themselves a pity party or blaming their lack of success on everything that has happened to them in life. Instead, they choose to make the best of each situation and remain faithful, no matter what.
- Dreamers keep themselves pure, no matter what is going on around them or what happens to them. They do not let sexual temptations sabotage their purpose. They run from

it, even if they have to run out of their clothes! So many dreamers are sabotaged by sexual temptations. If you want to receive the favor of God, like Joseph, you have to protect yourself from sexual sabotage. You have to run from it.

- Dreamers are not deterred by opposition. In many cases, your dream will not be understood or agreed with by those around you. Dreamers simply press forward to make their dream a reality.

- Dreamers know that it takes time for dreams to become reality. They are not instant-gratification people. They know, in many cases, it will be years before their dreams are realized. They persevere through trials and tribulation, knowing that it produces perseverance, proven character, and hope.

> *"Tribulation brings about perseverance; and perseverance, proven character; and proven character, hope."* [11]
> -*Romans 5:3-5*

- Dreamers are successful men and women.

- Dreamers are blessed beyond their wildest dreams! They reap the rewards of faithfulness, integrity, wisdom, and favor. They know whom the blessings are coming from and they keep every situation, good or bad, in that perspective.

- Dreamers are business-minded. People end up buying from dreamers. They use the wisdom from God to be entrepreneurial, creative, and even profitable to their employer. Joseph ultimately added extreme wealth to himself and Pharaoh, while at the same time making a difference in the lives of many.

- Dreamers are generous. They give of their time, talent, and money for the good of many. They do it from the heart. It's natural to them. It is not from hidden agendas or ulterior motives.
- Dreamers are forgivers. On their path to making their dreams reality, there are multiple opportunities to forgive!

On a side note, unforgiveness is a dream killer. It leads to nothing good. Forgive as you have been forgiven. Don't allow unforgiveness to sideline your dreams and prevent you from reaching your goal of being a true success.

In closing, John Maxwell has a great definition of a dream:

> *"Here is my definition of a dream that can be put to the test and pass: A dream is an inspiring picture of the future that energizes your mind, will, and emotions, empowering you to do everything you can to achieve it.*
>
> *A genuine dream is a picture and blueprint of a person's purpose and potential. Or as my friend Sharon Hull says, 'A dream is the seed of possibility planted in the soul of a human being, which calls him to pursue a unique PATH to the realization of his purpose'."* [12]

What's Your Dream?

Rosalie Jefferson

Rosalie Jefferson had been an entrepreneur most of her adult life. Although she worked in corporate America in a full-time capacity, it was seldom that she wasn't engaged in something in addition to her day job. A strong believer in not putting all of her eggs in one basket, she diversified her income portfolio by becoming a patented inventor, a life coach, a furniture store owner and a writer. She always had a dream of having a residual income that would allow her to live life on her terms. Rosalie had experience with network marketing and in her first venture, she had achieved the top position in her company. However, after 7 years she decided to put it to rest because although lucrative, there was no residual income involved, so essentially she found herself still trading hours for dollars.

In 2006, the Jefferson's family physician introduced Rosalie and her then husband, Robert, to a unique way of creating real residual income through network marketing. After a bit of arm-twisting, Rosalie realized the potential and dove in with both feet! In less than a month she promoted to the first leadership position in her company, and within 3 months, she had promoted again! However, the road going forward was a journey with many detours. In 2008, after a long marriage, Rosalie went through a difficult divorce. Ten months later, Rosalie's beloved Mom passed away. In less than one year, both of her anchors were gone and Rosalie was trying to make sense of everything. The flame that once burned so brightly for business began to extinguish.

Rosalie did virtually nothing with her network marketing business for well more than a year, but her income continued to thrive and her team steadily grew! During this time, Rosalie was also working as a Talent Agent for an International Speakers Bureau. With the Internet quickly eroding some of the income potential in that industry, she decided it made more sense to take the plunge and work her network marketing business full-time. She had seen the potential of network marketing the previous year and it gave her the confidence to pursue her dream. Without a doubt, her network marketing business had secured her future, afforded her the ability to bounce back after two major life losses, and provided her financial stability typically reserved for high salary earners, business owners, and entertainers who receive royalties. Today, Rosalie is a Residual Millionaire and loves helping others change their lives with residual income.

When I think back to my life and its humble beginnings, I shudder to think of God's amazing grace. Few people know that I taught my own mother how to drive when she was 46 years old. We never had a car when I grew up; as the youngest of 6 kids, it was all we could do to keep food on the table. So when I look in my garage today and see not one, but two paid for Mercedes Benzes, I am amazed and overwhelmed with gratitude! I feel compelled to share with others the magnitude and power of residual income through network marketing. I am always mindful that my job is to plant the seed. Whether the seed falls on stony or fertile soil is not my call to make. I leave the harvest to God. But, I take full responsibility for being the yielded vessel. Perhaps the next person will come along and water or fertilize it, but nothing grows without first planting the seed of residual income.

-Rosalie Jefferson

191

Residual Millionaire
Action Steps

Have you put your dreams on a back shelf? What's your dream? Have you been proactive in seeking wisdom and favor? What lessons did you learn from the story of Joseph?

1. Put your dream in writing.

2. Be committed to it and stay faithful at all costs.

3. Ask God for wisdom as you follow your dream and keep kindness and truth as ultimate priorities.

4. Chase your dream and change the world.

I hope this book has inspired you to dream. I also hope it leads you down the Residual Millionaire Path and helps you become a Residual Millionaire. But most importantly, I hope it leads you down the path to true success.

Believe in yourself and the fact that you were created to succeed. Believe in others. Decide to dream. Act on your dreams. Live on purpose. Change the world.

ACKNOWLEDGEMENTS

This book has been a long journey and there are many who played a part in making it happen. But, I first of all want to thank God for His extreme love for me.

To my girls, Lauren, Amy, and Meagan, you are my driving force. I could not ask for three better daughters. I am so proud of each of you and so blessed to be your dad. You have made me laugh, cry, scratch my head, clean my gun (only for the boys), question my ability to be a dad, made my life an adventure, and most importantly, made my life meaningful. I always smile when I think of each of you. You have inspired me and caused me to be a better man. Thank you for your love. I love you more than you will ever know.

To my parents, thank you for your commitment to God, to so many people, and to me. I simply would not be where I am today without your belief in me and your great example of the Christian life. Mom & Dad, THANK YOU! I love you very much and appreciate all the sacrifices you made and continue to make for me and for my family. Thank you for teaching me about life and what true success is all about.

To my sister, Susan, thank you for playing a huge role in my success and being one of my biggest fans. You're the best. I love you.

To my brothers, Scott and Stan, thank you for telling me I was adopted and showing me a picture of myself on the front cover of National Geographic! I still wonder to this day. Actually, thank you for being great examples to me.

A special thanks to Rob Snyder, Pierre Koshakji, Mark "Bouncer" Schiro, Doug Witt, Darryl Smith, Adrian Avila, Michael Tacker, Joe Natoli, Steve Florez, Joanna McQuien and your entire staffs, without whom my story may have been much different… Thank you!

A special thanks to Andy Brink, Louis Miori, Wendell Campbell, Alan Cantrell, and Brian Webb for pushing me and helping me to get this book done. Thank you for your friendship and your belief in me.

A special thanks to Presley Swagerty and Donny Anderson for inspiring me to higher levels and pushing me to be, do, and have so much more!

A special thanks to Jerry Scribner, Greg McCord, Randy Hedge, Mark Dean, Brian Lucia, Ryan Morris, Mark Florez, Trey Dyer, Tim Rose, Terry Yancey, Jay Veal, Elbert & Labeebah Thomas, Ralph & Andra Williams, Inge Saenz, Chad Williams, Martha Troy, and Randall Blackmon. Thank you for your leadership, example, friendship, and commitment. You each have played a huge role in my success and made an impact on my life.

A special thanks to my leaders: Susan Fisher, Bob & Sue Ledbetter, Bryan & Terri Hatch, Jim & Lori Spargur, Louis & Michelle Miori, Wendell & Amy Campbell, Sue Anderson & Nedim Oztan, Robert Bell & Linda Robinson, Alan & Linda Cantrell, Domenic & Wendy Carlucci, Willa Gipson, Quin Lloyd, Lisa Montgomery (and, of course, my good buddy, Byron Montgomery, who is now in a much better place), Melvin Farrell, Christina Patterson, Lang & Penny Smith, Steve & Michelle Reynolds, Scott & Lisa Stok, Ken & Joanne Langdon, Wes & Sunny Wessel, Manual Thomas, Lee & Lisa Cochran, Ron Woodall, Dr. Terry Young, and there are many others (too many to list, you know who you are). Thank you so much for the role you have played in my success. I simply would not be where I am today without all of you, your hard work, and your leadership. I am forever grateful.

Notes

CHAPTER 1

1. Robert Rosenthal and Lenore Jacobson, "Teachers' Expectancies: Determinants of Pupils' IQ Gains", Psychological Reports 19 (1966): 115-118; and Pygmalion in the Classroom: Teacher Expectation and Pupils' Intellectual Development (New York: Crown, 2003)
2. http://www.ziglar.com/newsletter/november-1-2011-edition-44
3. "Napoleon Hill." BrainyQuote.com. Xplore Inc, 2013. 17 June 2013. http://www.brainyquote.com/quotes/quotes/n/napoleonhi393807.html
4. "John Hancock." BrainyQuote.com. Xplore Inc, 2013. 17 June 2013. http://www.brainyquote.com/quotes/quotes/j/johnhancoc142583.html
5. "John C. Maxwell." BrainyQuote.com. Xplore Inc, 2013. 17 June 2013. http://www.brainyquote.com/quotes/quotes/j/johncmaxw380196.html
6. "Zig Ziglar." BrainyQuote.com. Xplore Inc, 2013. 17 June 2013. http://www.brainyquote.com/quotes/quotes/z/zigziglar173502.html
7. Proverbs 10:22 NASB
8. "John Andrew Holmes." BrainyQuote.com. Xplore Inc, 2013. 17 June 2013. http://www.brainyquote.com/quotes/quotes/j/johnandrew105928.html
9. Proverbs 3:5-6 NASB
10. Jeremiah 9:24 NASB

CHAPTER 2

1. "Jim Rohn." Challenge To Succeed audio series
2. Proverbs 11:14

CHAPTER 5

1. "General Norman Schwarzkopf" http://theveteranssite.greatergood.com/clickToGive/vet/article/General-Norman-Schwarzkopf-Dies-Age-78-December-27-2012821

2. "Michael Jordan." BrainyQuote.com. Xplore Inc, 2013. 18 June 2013. http://www.brainyquote.com/quotes/quotes/m/michaeljor167380.html

3. "Jan Jarvis, (2012, February 5) Marathon man. Ft. Worth Star Telegram, pp. 1E and 6E

4. "Jan Jarvis, (2012, February 5) Marathon man. Ft. Worth Star Telegram, pp. 1E and 6E

CHAPTER 6

1. "Stephen R. Covey." http://thinkexist.com/quotation/opposition_is_a_natural_part_of_life-just_as_we/8347.html

2. http://www.dsa.org/research/industry-statistics/

CHAPTER 7

1. "Tony Robbins." BrainyQuote.com. Xplore Inc, 2013. 18 June 2013. http://www.brainyquote.com/quotes/quotes/t/tonyrobbin134116.html

2. Luke 14:28 NASB

3. Proverbs 21:5 NASB

4. James 4:15 NASB

5. Proverbs 16:9 NASB

6. Matthew 6:33 NASB

7. Proverbs 6:6-11 NASB

8. "Jon Acuff." Start

9. "John Maxwell." The 15 Laws of Growth

CHAPTER 9

1. "Thomas A. Edison." BrainyQuote.com. Xplore Inc, 2013. 18 June 2013. www.brainyquote.com/quotes/quotes/t/thomasaed132683.html
2. "Herb Kelleher." http://www.brandautopsy.com/2012/03/herb-kelleher-on-strategic-planning.html

CHAPTER 10

1. "John Maxwell." The 15 Laws of Growth
2. "Bill Gates." BrainyQuote.com. Xplore Inc, 2013. 18 June 2013. www.brainyquote.com/quotes/quotes/b/billgates173262.html

CHAPTER 12

1. "Danny Thomas." BrainyQuote.com. Xplore Inc, 2013. 18 June 2013. www.brainyquote.com/quotes/quotes/d/dannythoma187291.html
2. "Dwight D. Eisenhower." BrainyQuote.com. Xplore Inc, 2013. 18 June 2013. www.brainyquote.com/quotes/quotes/d/dwightdei101562.html
3. "Edwin Louis Cole." Power of Potential
4. "Bill Gates." BrainyQuote.com. Xplore Inc, 2013. 18 June 2013. www.brainyquote.com/quotes/quotes/b/billgates385136.html

CHAPTER 13

1. "Tony Robbins." BrainyQuote.com. Xplore Inc, 2013. 18 June 2013. www.brainyquote.com/quotes/quotes/t/tonyrobbin132984.html
2. "Jim Rohn." BrainyQuote.com. Xplore Inc, 2013. 18 June 2013. www.brainyquote.com/quotes/quotes/j/jimrohn132691.html
3. Sarnataro, Barbara Russi. "Top 10 Fitness Facts" WebMD. May 14, 2008. (July 20, 2010) http://www.webmd.com/fitness-exercise/guide/exercise-benefits

CHAPTER 14

1. "Norman Schwarzkopf." BrainyQuote.com. Xplore Inc, 2013. 19 June 2013. www.brainyquote.com/quotes/quotes/n/normanschw163145.html
2. Proverbs 22:1 NASB
3. Proverbs 19:1 NASB
4. Romans 12:18 NASB
5. "John Maxwell." The 21 Irrefutable Laws of Leadership
6. Proverbs 11:3 NASB

CHAPTER 15

1. "Zig Ziglar." BrainyQuote.com. Xplore Inc, 2013. 19 June 2013. www.brainyquote.com/quotes/quotes/z/zigziglar173503.html
2. I Timothy 6:9 NASB
3. I Timothy 6:10 NASB
4. Matthew 6:19 NASB
5. "Billy Graham." BrainyQuote.com. Xplore Inc, 2013. 19 June 2013. www.brainyquote.com/quotes/quotes/b/billygraha150662.html

6. Matthew 6:24 NASB
7. Mark 8:36 NASB
8. Proverbs 23:5 NASB
9. Matthew 13:22 NASB

10. James 1:25 NASB
11. Deuteronomy 8:14-17 NAS, Psalms 10:4 NASB
12. Deuteronomy 8:18 NASB
13. Proverbs 10:4 NASB
14. Proverbs 6:6-11 NASB
15. Proverbs 14:23-24 NASB
16. Proverbs 14:23-24 NASB
17. Proverbs 22:9 NASB
18. James 3:16 NASB
19. Job 42 (The story of Job)

20. Proverbs 23:21 NASB
21. Proverbs 3:9-10, Malachi 3:8-12 NASB
22. Haggai 2:8 NASB
23. I Timothy 6:17-19 NASB
24. Proverbs 11:4

CHAPTER 16

1. Genesis 37:8 NASB
2. Genesis 39:2-3 NASB
3. Genesis 39:7 NASB
4. Genesis 39:21 NASB
5. Proverbs 3:13-16 NASB
6. James 1:5 NASB
7. Proverbs 3:1-4 NASB
8. U.S. Department of State, Bureau of Public Affairs (2003). "The Great Seal of the United States" <www.state.gov>. Retrieved 11-25-2011.
9. Bureau of Engraving, Currency Notes
10. U.S. Treasury (2010). "Portraits & Designs" www.treasury.gov Retrieved 11-25-2011.
11. Romans 5:3-5
12. "John Maxwell." Put Your Dream To The Test